CW00663388

Leonard Low was born in
He moved to London in 1   , ..c.c he was involved in building trade management for the next 23
years. He has two children, a huge ginger cat called
Hamish, a black dog called Lucifer and a rare breed
of hens — Scots Dumpys — to look after. A long fas-
cination with the dark side of history led to his first
book, *The Weem Witch*, which is now in its third
printing. Further books called *Largo's Untold Stories*
and *St Andrews' Untold Stories* revealed more obscure,
dark secrets, this time from his home village of
Largo and the town of St Andrews. A lecturer on the
subject of his books and the witch trials in general,
Lenny is a witch historian with many artefacts from
actual trials and a library full of 17th and 18th
century books for his source material. Lenny lives in
Leven with his partner Ruth, and stepdaughter
Amber.

Lenny says, 'Still an East Fife supporter, but we
need to win some games!'

By the same author

The Weem Witch
There Are Such Things!
Largo's Untold Stories
St Andrews' Untold Stories

THE BATTLE

OF

ST MONANS

LEONARD LOW

Steve Savage
LONDON AND EDINBURGH

Steve Savage Publishers Ltd
The Old Truman Brewery
91 Brick Lane
LONDON
E1 6QL

www.savagepublishers.com

First published in Great Britain by Steve Savage Publishers Ltd 2017

ISBN: 978-1-904246-46-6

Typeset by Steve Savage Publishers
Printed and bound by SRP Ltd, Exeter

Contents

Introduction

This is a subject I have wanted to research in depth for a long time. In 2005, when I was researching a Fife witch trial, I happened upon a paragraph in *The Shores of Fife*, a book from 1872 by William Ballingal. While discussing the history of the Fife village of St Monans, the book described the actions of an admiral in the English navy: "Lord Clinton landed from an English fleet no less than 1,200 men on the beach at St Monance ... his army was repulsed by the strength of Fife, which mustered here in numbers, and fought with great gallantry".

That was it! The briefest of information on what seems to have been a major engagement that had taken place on the beaches of St Monans on 19 June 1548. But to my amazement, Ballingal treated the incident so casually and appeared so offhand. In just a paragraph, he told of the manhood of Fife fighting the invader back to the seas, just as the Veniconi Picts had done on this coastline, fighting against Roman and Viking armies in the past. I made it my goal to explore and expand further what could be found of this story. I had to spend weeks on end searching for any information and trailing through official letters written from 1548 onwards from English, French and Scots records. But with time, including hundreds of hours searching through dusty old records, I have found enough that has been written of the battle to give the reader an in-depth view of the fighting and the struggle that took place here on the beaches of St Monans.

It is a battle that has been lost to history – and today I try to bring it back as it happened, and to find out the reasons for it being so forgotten. Anyone who knows me will know I'm a passionate historian. I find the unpleasant side of history fascinating, as readers of my previous work and audiences at many lectures will testify. What irks me is history as rich as this being forgotten and ignored. Men dying in their hundreds were to be misplaced in history, and all that was left recording them was word of mouth and a few paragraphs in old books.

The Benedictine monastery of Abercrombie (which is now St Monans church) was fired on and burned in 1544 by the English from a distance, secure in the safety of their grand naval fleet. The monks were to repair and rebuild the damage, but the building would be emptied again twelve years from the date of the battle as the wheels of the Reformation turned in 1559. The monks were chased from the priory and replaced by Protestant sympathisers.

It was in the monastery that I could have expected the deeds of valour from the 1548 battle to have been recorded in great detail, giving the names and exploits of heroism on the part of its victors. The monks were the most literate of people in those dark days. But all the files and diaries that could have informed us about the battle have been lost with the chaos of the following years. The monastery is surely the place where the victors would have thanked and praised God for the victory. For this effort to be forgotten and lost is an utter tragedy.

It is time we resurrected this piece of history, and I hope that with this book the tourist will have something more to view and ponder over in this lovely wee burgh. As with the Pittenweem witches I championed in my book *The Weem Witch*, nothing exists for the tourist in St Monans to learn of our rich history, no monument, not even a simple plaque.

It is time we recognized our ancestors for what were seen in their own time as their achievements and – in the case of the Pittenweem witches – their failures.

Author's thanks

Love to these great people – Bruce Marshall, John Vandieken, David Baxter, Jamie (up the Rams), Roj Wilson, Irish Jocky, Willie Maclean and Cath and Walter, Cousin Brenda, Anya and Hugh Mackay, Ian Muirhead, and Steve Gilfeather.

Brian Watson was a lovely man, never shy with a dram, a man with a thousand stories and a well lived-in face, weather-beaten by his years in the merchant navy. He kindly let me photo his finds

Leonard Low not far from the site of the battle.

from his metal-detecting days. Sadly he died in 2013.

Thanks to Mrs Proudfoot for information on her digs around the ruins of Newark Castle. Dave Low and Linda Whiteford, my brother and sister, for help in finding books, and my two little big ones Callum and Kirsty Low. And not forgetting my step-daughter Amber Sinclair-Case. Many thanks again to Steve Savage for giving me a fourth chance to work with him with this book. Continued thanks to these magazines and newspapers that have supported my work: the *East Fife Mail*, the *Courier* in Dundee, the *Sun*, the *Evening Standard*, the *Weekly News*, *Haunted Magazine*, *Fortean Times* and many more.

There's an amazing lady in my life who puts up with my eccentricities. I'm hard work, and I work very unsociable hours, sometimes days on end without sleep. I disappear into ruined and haunted buildings for my magazine, coming home covered in dust from head to toe and suffering from severe man flu all the time, while she puts up with a massive ginger cat called Hamish that bites everybody except his Dad, but somehow through all my chaos she puts up with me – Ruth Sinclair. I sincerely mean it when I say I couldn't write this stuff without you by my side ... x

Chapter One

The Place

St Monans sits on the coastline of the Firth of Forth, nestling between Elie to the west and Pittenweem to the east not far away.

The village of St Monans was named after St Monan, but he is an extremely hazy figure. There is one legend that says he was a missionary who came from the continent with some Hungarians led by St Adrian. The historian Boethius says that they were probably not Hungarians but from Ireland or Northern England. There was an Irish bishop called St Moinenno with the same feast day as St Monan (1st March). Some have even suggested that St Adrian left Ireland with St Moinenno's relics and this was confused with St Monan.

The name Monan is an affectionate version of the saint's name. This happens with Irish saints, and is shown by the fact that it begins with *'mo'*, the Gaelic for 'my'.

Legend tells us that St Monan's life was brutally cut short when he died on the Isle of May (just in view from St Monans). He arrived there in 832 and was murdered by Viking invaders about 841 when they ransacked the island, killing hundreds of the monks who had settled there.

Other than the version in the book *Breviarium Aberdonense*, which dates back to the early 16th century, we really know very little about St Monan. His relics were brought back from the Isle of May by his supporters and interred and worshipped at the chapel he had formed. The area soon took his name.

The parish church has stood here since the middle of the 14th century. The parish went under the name Abercrombie till 1646, when the congregation stopped using the now ruined kirk at Abercrombie (inland from St Monans) and switched to the church at St Monans. The village went by the name St Monans or is written in old accounts as Monanus, St Monance or St Menin.

The church was founded by David II (Robert the Bruce's son) in the fortieth year of his reign. The medieval historian Froissart says that this was n gratitude to St Monan, after praying for the moval of an arrow barb which he had taken in e head at the battle of Neville's Cross in England

The ancient kirk of St Monans still stands close to the sea.

in 1346. But according to the *Scotichronicon*, he set up the church for a different reason – after being saved from a shipwreck. The majestic building we see today is the result of this, but it is thought an earlier religious settlement was here before that, perhaps set up by St Monan himself.

The two villages of Abercrombie and St Monans lie close to each other; the village of Abercrombie was once a most populous village, mostly a farming community with a small quantity of lime and iron works, but the harbour of St Monans has taken its inhabitants away from here and it is now the bigger of the two.

Sir John Connell's *Treatise on Tithes* tells us that Abercrombie has been a parish as far back as 1174, and that the church is obviously of very great antiquity. It was abandoned in 1646 when the parishes of Abercrombie and St Monance became one. The church of St Monance, situated on the shore, now serves the united parish.

Abercrombie parish kirk is now a roofless ruin in which the author recently spent some time. It is a pleasant retreat for a visit, and the grass is kept well-trimmed and respectable. But history or legend dictates that this little church was the scene of a hellish freak of nature, and the following tale gives the horrid story.

About the middle of the twelfth century the estate of Sir Humphrey Abercrombie, who did not have a son, was inherited by his two daughters, Mary and Margaret. They were young and unmarried and attracted the attention of neighbouring knights and such as were of the same high class as themselves.

The elder girl, Mary, had a certain strength and self-reliance, while the younger girl, Margaret, was graceful and gentle with a soft and placid character and a rare beauty. Although the sisters were unlike in mind and features, they set their eyes and hearts on one person. Both high-souled

Mary and shrinking, soft-eyed Margaret fell for their cousin, the soldier Philip de Candela.

He was a member of a Norman family that settled at Anstruther some time after 1066, and were the feudal lords of Anstruther, eventually taking Anstruther as their surname.

Margaret was chosen to be Philip de Candela's bride, and it is said that they were married by the hermit St Monan (unlikely, if St Monan really lived in the 9th century).

The disappointed loser in love, Margaret's sister Mary, cursed the happy couple bitterly, and vowed undying hatred to both of them. Whatever sisterly feelings she had once held were now totally defunct and she brooded deep in her castle of Abercrombie.

Six months after the wedding, war broke out between King Stephen, the usurper of the English throne, and his cousin and competitor, Matilda, the daughter of King Henry I of England. In this contest, Margaret's husband was among the first to join the standard of King David of Scotland, who supported Matilda's claim. The conflict between David and Stephen went on to have a peaceful ending, and a treaty between the two kings, signed at Durham, gave David more land. However Philip de Candela had been sent south into

England, where he was killed in a mere skirmish that happened by chance.

Now the two sisters reconciled their friendship over de Candela's death, turning to the church to seek a priestly advisor. The two women decided to set up a church to absolve them of their grief, and so they set up the church at Abercrombie dedicated to St Mary and St Margaret.

There Bishop Arnold of St Andrews met them, and in the church he had the two sisters kneel before the altar to show their reconciliation in the sight of God. As the bishop leaned forward to give his blessing, there was a mighty flash of vivid lightning, and a peal of thunder crashed upon the roof of the building.

There was a deep silence, an almost audible calm. Most of the congregation lay on the paved floor. Margaret and Mary were still kneeling upon the altar steps with buried heads and clasped hands. Bishop Arnold folded his hands upon the kneeling sisters, and bade them rise. There was no answer, whether by word or gesture, for the sisters were as dead as most the congregation, killed by the lightning strike that had smashed through the roof of the church.

In the reign of James III (1451–88) the St Monans church was gifted to the Blackfriars monks. The monks held ownership of the church when it was attacked by the English in 1544. With the coming of the Reformation, the monks were replaced in 1559, and around 1646 it became a parish church. According to the reports of the 1791 *Statistical Account of Scotland*, the church was much dilapidated, with the roof in a ruinous state in 1772. Eighteenth-century building projects have preserved what is now a rare example of a magnificent gothic church.

With its closeness to the sea, rising 21st-century tides are proving a hazard for this parish's existence. In the 1791 *Statistical Account of Scotland*, it is stated that the soil in the area was very fertile and manageable with little clay. Sea kelp was regularly harvested and used as high-quality manure on the fields. The farms' main crops were peas, beans and cabbages, and the area had an abundance of coal works and at least nine salt-pans, from which the sea salt was taken to Pittenweem harbour where it was used for curing fish and also exported. It is said it took five tonnes of coal to be burned for every tonne of salt made, boiling down the sea water in massive metal pans. When salt deposits which could be mined were found in England, it became too expensive to produce the salt here. The remains of the nine salt-pan

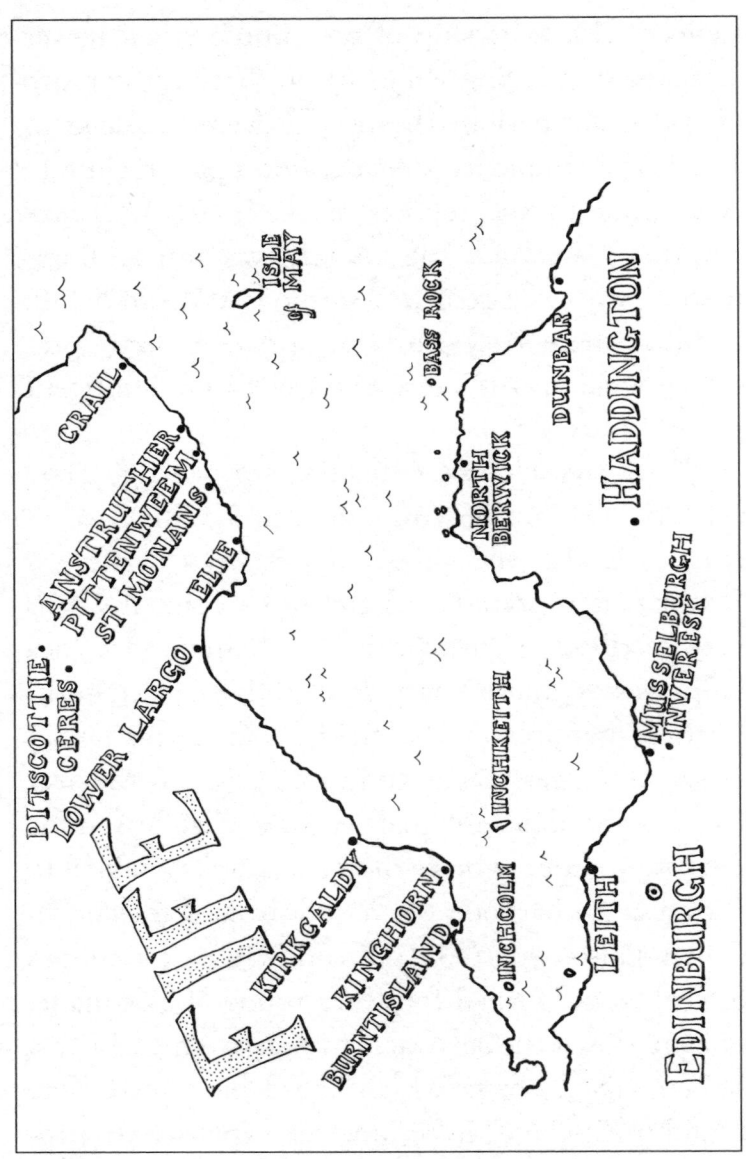

Map showing Fife, the Firth of Forth and the location of the village of St Monans.

houses can still be viewed along the coastal walk between St Monans and Pittenweem today.

St Monans is situated upon a spot with a triangular shape, one side of which verges upon the Firth of Forth, while the other two are sheltered by high rising grounds. The harbour in 16th-century reports was of no great significance, but what was noted was the great depth of water — between six and seven metres deep at the entrance. The harbour does not extend far out to sea and has a narrow entrance, which was noted as difficult and dangerous. From the earliest *Statistical Account*, the population in 1791 was 780; that would have included a big increase because of the mining operation that was thriving, with good seams of coal found.

In the years from 1544 to 1548 which we cover in this book, we have to imagine the population would have been under five hundred people in the village. In 1783, when the records start, there were 36 births registered in the year and 25 deaths.

The village is also described as having twelve taverns in the 18th century: today it has just the one, and that is only open part time!

St Monans has a history ingrained deep in the fishing trade, herring, cod and mackerel being the main catches. Fish was once taken by boat in

View towards St Monans showing the kirk spire in the distance.

huge amounts and traded at busy markets in Edinburgh.

According to John Jack's *History of St Monance*, around 1622 there were five or six "creers" (small trading vessels) that sailed regularly from this port to Orkney to take part in the herring fishing. Each crew consisted of ten expert able-bodied men; barrels of salt were carried with them and they lodged, victualled and cured their herrings in their own vessels. Smaller boats would stay at home and keep up the haddock fishing with lines and cod. When a boat returned from fishing it laid its catch out and divided it equally per man and one share for the boat's upkeep.

This was a trade that once had twenty boats in the port, which have now all vanished, leaving its harbour empty but for the crab fishermen and the pleasure boats. All the heavy industry has gone, as well as the dozen public houses it once had. But anyone visiting the place will be taken aback by what it has to offer in its natural beauty and surroundings.

The prominent gothic-looking church is set very close to the sea, separated by a wall. With rising tides causing concern, we had better appreciate what is here before coastal erosion finally takes its toll. It is a 14th-century stone building, solid looking with a strange roof like a witches' hat, rising to a spire*. It overlooks the

* NOTE: Indeed the church spire resembles a witches' hat in its shape ... and history tells of at least three of these creatures found in this parish as witches – in 1644 Betty Dote was found in the parish, taken to Pittenweem, where she was held in the Tolbooth and tortured ... before long she was joined by her sister Christian Dote and three Pittenweem witches: all were burned in the priory gardens. In 1651 Maggie Morgan was discovered, she was tortured in the town house. A brief trial was held and she was burnt at the stake, just behind where the church stands today. Her remains and ashes were bagged up and emptied upon the rim of this witches'-hat steeple, to be blown into consecrated ground. There is mention of another witch Tibbie Dowie of around 1548 in John Jack's book *History of St Monance* (1844), but there is no other history to her. Maggie's story and that of the Dote sisters is told in more detail in my book *The Weem Witch*.

The ruined state of Newark Castle in the 1800s.

The remains of historic Newark Castle as they survive today.

North Sea with the empty concave harbour completing the calendar-like setting for a picture of stillness and beauty. Behind the church by a few hundred metres lies the ruined castle of Newark, which from 1649 was home to the famous Scottish general David Leslie. The sea has started to reclaim this old building. It is down here on the beach that our story is based.

Like the Pittenweem witches, it is another piece of Scottish history that has been forgotten and lost.

It's bad enough that no plaque or board is set up to give our visitors to the castle any information whatsoever on what they are looking at and the history of the great Lord Newark – David Leslie – who once lived here (a hundred years after this forgotten battle). But his place in the history books is safe, for what he achieved on the battlefields.

Born in Scotland around 1600, David Leslie was a man who fought for the Swedish crown as well as the Russian royal court; he arrived back and fought in the Civil War on the same side as Cromwell. After taking part in the battle of Marston Moor, he fought in Scotland against the royalists and defeated General Montrose at Philiphaugh in 1646, catching his depleted forces and ending Montrose's

The coast near Dunbar as depicted in an old engraving.

run of six straight victories over the government troops. With Montrose beaten, Charles I's last chance of power was gone. Leslie led the fight with, and then against Oliver Cromwell in the civil wars of 1642–50, losing his last fight at Dunbar where he had Cromwell trapped on a beach, but was overruled by religious leaders. They led the Scottish army down from the heights waving crosses which they apparently believed would ward off the evil English ... it ended as a massacre. Leslie's final battle was at Worcester in 1650, where Cromwell finally smashed resistance and any support left for Charles II.

After Cromwell's death, however, the fortunes of the monarchy revived. Released from the Tower of London after the 1660 Restoration of Charles II, Leslie was given the title Lord Newark.

Today, standing and looking at Newark Castle, the tourist has no choice but to find that information on General Leslie themselves later, at home or in libraries if they want to search hard enough, as there's nothing to provide any history of the place here.

But it is next to this castle on the land and beach where my story starts. This was where nearly five hundred years ago the local lairds banded together and fought a common enemy. The numbers to this fight are not completely clear – we only know the English army's overall strength, and that only approximately – in some reports that was 5,000 men. The Scots in one area of the fighting had 120 men; the local laird Sir James Sandilands, who lived in Newark Castle, had an unnumbered amount of armed fishermen and peasants involved in the fighting; but the main strength came via St Andrews and the Prior there, Lord James Stewart. Their contribution is not numbered, but may have been as many as 1,000 men.

It's incredible and appalling that this event has been totally forgotten, but a mighty battle was fought and won by local Scottish lairds who banded themselves against an old foe and won a brave and gallant victory despite all the odds against them. It was fought around the beach here in the year 1548. It was fought against the English who landed here by their Admiral's direction under leadership of Lord Clinton, and were heavily defeated by an army directed by James Stewart, King James V's illegitimate son and half-brother of Mary Queen of Scots, and the men of Sir John Wemyss. The battle left between six and nine hundred of the enemy dead on St Monans beach and many others drowned.

We find with the victors of battle, that exaggeration of the fallen is not unusual: in some historical reports of war there are more slain than actually took part! But some of my sources come from English writers also, and some of them claim the English dead as high as nine hundred! Yet this sweeping victory isn't anywhere in the history books or Scotland's roll of military honour.

Think of other battlefields in Scotland. In Falkirk, where Bonnie Prince Charlie's Highlanders fought and won against the government force in 1746, there is a monument and it has its place in the history books, but the dead on the field were only 350. At the battle of Solway Moss in 1542, James V's army, commanded by his favourite Oliver Sinclair, lost twenty men confronting the English forces, who lost seven men. The Scottish force there numbered 15,000 but they hated Oliver Sinclair and refused to fight for him. No monarch fought in that affair, but it has its place in the history books, the defeat in battle contributing to James V's death from a broken heart. These are two of many examples where an engagement of forces resulted in minimal numbers of slain but a memorial stands to record the deeds, and they have their place in the history books.

Why is there nothing in St Monans to celebrate this great victory that was fought here? With the numbers fighting it was no brief little skirmish. I can't quite understand why history like this is not highlighted, especially in places like St Monans, where all the heavy industry that was once here, such as the boat building, coal mining and fishing, has gone, and tourism is now the only lifeblood of the village. I made it my goal to find out why this fight has been forgotten and wiped from Scottish history.

A recent tourist guide in St Monans was not very positive in his comments on this area, finding the church was closed and museum shut! "A scenic lump of stone" is how it was described. All the attractions that were on offer in the town were also closed! His review was compiled on a Friday in May, the height of the summer trade! There was no butcher to be seen, no shoe shop and no hardware store. The only café was shut! Tourists with glum disappointment written on their faces were found walking around aimlessly, wondering what kind of backwater place they had stumbled into.

The review I can have sympathy with. It is probably upsetting to the locals for its chastising of the place, but I was recently told by a local man that out of all the houses by the seafront only seven are now occupied, the rest are holiday cottages! As a tourist here myself, my trip to the castle arouses in me the same disbelief that no plaque gives any information to the tourist about what they are looking at! And it is meant to be a coastal walk-way! Tourism has to be the lifeblood of these small towns now, but come on town chiefs, give the tourists something to see here! At present there's nothing. I hope that my rendition of the battle, from the sources written about the struggle, will make the reader study this area a little more closely, and the people of St Monans stand a little prouder for the brave deeds their ancestors achieved in defence of their own little town.

Scotland was never shy about defending its shores, and the bravery and the actions against Romans, Vikings and Saxons are recorded in many a manuscript and book, but I promise you there is nothing much mentioning the heroics of what happened in the battle of St Monans.

Now ask yourself why this is so? The *Gazetteer of Scotland*, printed in 1844, sits in my library – a fine two-volume book giving intimate details of every village and town in Scotland ... it has nothing at all on the battle.

Another book in my collection, the 1791 *Statistical Account of Scotland*, Vol X, *Fife*, again has nothing of the fight on the beaches of St Monans. I have dozens of other first-edition source books on the Kingdom of Fife, volumes printed in the 18th and 19th centuries, but again nothing!

Light is perhaps thrown on the mystery of the vanished battle by an author called James Anderson, writing in 1727 the first of his three volumes of the life of Mary Queen of Scots (*Collections relating to the History of Mary Queen of Scots*). He starts off his first volume with an apology ... in his research through the Scottish archives he finds that large tracts of records are seemingly lost – from the years of 1547, 1548 and 1551 when the Regents Mar, Morton and Lennox ruled, and some more in Mary Queen of Scots' reign. The villain of the piece for these lost records – that may well have included details of the battle of St Monans and the lost records from St Monans parish – is Oliver Cromwell. He in 1650 transported all the Scottish records to the "safekeeping" of the Tower of London. When King Charles II was restored to the throne ten years later in 1660, the records were returned. They were sent by sea, but because of bad weather some of them were transferred to another ship (the *Elizabeth* of Burntisland) which came to grief and sank off the coast of Newcastle with 85 large barrels of Scottish records, that were lost in the sea forever.

The official parish and monastery records could be missing due to the mayhem that the monasteries suffered in the Reformation years leading up to 1560. And a hundred years from that date in 1660 a ship possibly sank with them off the English coast. One way or the other, the records are not there ... to discover what happened I have to go to writings from after the battle.

In the writings of John Lesley, Bishop of Ross, (1527–96) we find a writer who seems to have spoken to witnesses or witnessed the action himself.

Chapter Two

The Participants

The English participants...

The Seymours

The events in St Monans and Montrose in June 1548 involved powerful figures from both sides of the Border. On the English side two Seymour brothers played a part: Admiral Thomas Seymour, and Edward Seymour, Duke of Somerset.

Edward Seymour was born in 1500, and was the older brother of Thomas, who was born in 1508. They were the sons of John Seymour and Margaret Wentworth, and grew up at Wulfhall, the Seymour family home in Wiltshire in south-west England.

Edward rose to power when Henry VIII married his sister Jane in 1536 and he was created the Earl of Hertford and became "Warden of the Scottish Marches". He devastated southern

Kings of England: Henry VIII and his son, Edward VI.

Scotland in the war known as the "rough wooing" and defeated the Scots at the battle of Pinkie in September 1547.

Having been chosen as the Lord Protector (regent) of England after the death of Henry VIII in 1547, Edward created himself the Duke of Somerset. The new king, Edward VI, was still a boy, and only ten years old, and Somerset's role was to govern England during his nephew Edward VI's childhood years.

Like Edward, his younger brother Thomas Seymour owed his position to being a brother of the English queen Jane Seymour who had been the third wife of Henry VIII and mother to Edward VI. This was the case even though Jane Seymour died in 1537.

King Henry VIII had finally died towards the end of January 1547. The scheming Thomas Seymour quickly married his widow Catherine Parr, becoming her fourth husband. This happened in April. Many court members thought this ridiculously too soon after King Henry's death and despised Thomas for his lust to power. Thomas had been made Admiral of the English Fleet in 1544 at the time of the "rough wooing". A close friend, Sir Nicholas Throakmorton, decribed Thomas Seymour in a letter as "a forceful and reckless man, very attractive to the ladies and hardy liberal and wise".

Admiral Seymour was under orders from Edward the Duke of Somerset, his brother, to harass Scottish and French transport vessels.

Lord Clinton

Lord Edward Clinton was born in Scrivelsby, Lincolnshire in 1512. He succeeded his father Thomas Clinton as the 9th Baron of Clinton. In 1532 he joined Henry VIII at the siege of Boulogne, then served in the English navy in the wars of 1544–48. He commanded the English navy during Edward Seymour's invasion of Scotland in 1547.

Nicholas Poyntz

Born in 1510, Nicholas came from a Gloucestershire family. His grandfather had been Sir Robert Poyntz, Chancellor to Catherine of Aragon (Henry VIII's first wife). During the "rough wooing" (1543–1550), Poyntz commanded the *Great Galley*, a warship. In 1544, Edward Seymour sent Nicholas Poyntz to burn Kinghorn and other towns in Fife.

The Scottish participants in the St Monans and Montrose landings:

James Stewart (Earl of Moray)

James was a member of the House of Stewart. The illegitimate son of James V, born in 1531, he was one of James V's five children to be born out of wedlock. His mother was Margaret Erskine. He supported his half-sister Mary Queen of Scots in the tender years of her reign.

Lord James Stewart was stationed at St Andrews as its Prior in 1548. When news of the imminent invasion at St Monans reached him, his reaction was instant: he gathered the manhood of St Andrews available to him, collecting more men to him through the parishes of Balmungo, Pitmillie and Lathockerd to speed the eight miles to St Monans by horse. With his prestigious name on the field of battle, in many accounts he is given full credit for the victory. (But much credit must be given to Sir John Wemyss and the men of Largo, for they developed the tactics of the fight and led the battle from the start to encourage the English to attack.)

Andrew and John Wood

Andrew was the first son of the famed admiral Sir Andrew Wood. He was one of three sons and a daughter left by the great admiral when he died around 1515. He would inherit the castle of Largo after his father's death and was witness to the death of King James V in 1542.

Another son was John, who studied theology at St Leonard's College at St Andrews University, and no doubt knew James Stewart (the half-brother of Mary Queen of Scots) who was Prior. When the fires were lit on the hills around the Scottish coast, warning of imminent English invasion, the fire on the summit of Largo Law (over 300 metres high) would have been easily seen from Castle Largo.

Along with the men of Sir John Wemyss, Andrew Wood of Largo Castle gathered his retainers and seasoned fighters from his father

Admiral Sir Andrew Wood's exploits and made haste to the spot where the English were landing. John, studying at St Andrews, would have accompanied James Stewart's host leaving in haste for St Monans but I imagine him fighting alongside his kinsmen and his brother on the field.

John Erskine of Dun

Born in Angus in 1509, John Erskine was a friend of reformers such as George Wishart and John Knox. At the time of the assault by the English on Montrose beach in 1548, Erskine was Provost of Montrose and High Constable, a position his grandfather had held before him.

Sir James Sandilands

Sir James Sandilands of Cruivie was the owner of Newark Castle. In 1547 Mary of Guise (the widow of James V) proposed to her lords of state to raise funds for a standing professional army in Scotland. The money was to be raised by more taxes and was very unpopular. It was Sir James Sandilands and Sir John Wemyss who took the news to the Queen Mother that it was an unpopular decision. She took on board her loyal men's wishes.

Sir John Wemyss

The family of Wemyss originates from the family of MacDuff – Maormor of Fife during the reign of Malcolm Canmore, 1058–93. The Wemyss family is one of the very few lowland families which can lay claim to a Celtic bloodline. The land here used to belong to Macduff, high constable of Scotland from Shakespeare's *Macbeth*!

Sir John Wemyss, the eldest son of Sir David Wemyss and Katherine Sinclair, was born around 1513. He married twice, to Margaret Otterburn and Janet Trail. He had been asked by Parliament to intercept an English invasion into Scotland in July 1547, but when he reached Peebles he obtained a disposition allowing a number of his men to return to Castle Wemyss his homestead in case of attack, as the English armada was working its way along the Fife coastline.

At the battle of Pinkie, which was fought on 10th September 1547, Wemyss had a Fife regiment fighting for the Regent Arran, and during the rout he was taken prisoner on the field. But his captivity did not last long, as by the intervention of the Earl of Huntley, who became security for payment of Sir John Wemyss' ransom, the prisoners stationed at Newcastle were soon liberated. Wemyss had only one intention and that was to get back into the fight against the English again.

In *The Memorials of the Family of Wemyss* his activity against the enemy is mentioned:

"The laird was present at the siege of Broughty Castle in December of the same year (1547). In the following year the war was continued, and on 21st August he was required by letter from the queen to remain upon the south coasts of Fife for resisting the English. In connection with this commission the laird greatly distinguished himself in the valiant repulse of a large body of English soldiers who attempted to effect a landing at St. Monans on the Fifeshire coast."

The book also quotes from Lesley's *History of Scotland* and compares his account with other accounts such as Buchanan's.

Chapter Three

The Auld Alliance with France

The Auld Alliance with France was first formed in 1295 in the reign of King John Balliol of Scotland and King Phillip of France. The treaty was an agreement for the two countries to support each other if attacked by England.

This was an alliance that would have legions of men from both countries shedding blood on foreign soil in honour of this agreement for the next five centuries.

King Robert the Bruce would strengthen the treaty again at the height of his powers in 1326 with the Treaty of Corbeil. Again, it was renewed in 1371 by the Bishop of Glasgow on behalf of King Robert II of Scotland to the French King Charles V. In the following English invasion of France under Henry V, resulting in his famous victory at Agincourt in 1415, the Scots honoured the alliance, sending some 15,000 men to aid France against the aggressive English just as the French were at their lowest point. Under the Earl of Buchan the Scots won a resounding victory near the Castle of Baugé over the English, who were led by King Henry V's brother, the Duke of Clarence. He had been left in charge of the English forces (10,000 strong) as Henry his brother went home to England.

The Scottish chronicler Walter Bower in his book *Scotichronicon* describes in detail the fighting. Like William Wallace's victory in 1297 the action was contested over a bridge...

The Earl of Buchan feared the clever tricks of his enemies and sent Sir John Stewart Lord of Darnley his kinsman with a Frenchman, the Sire of Fountaines, and four hundred picked men to scout out the English. After suddenly coming upon the English force, the scouting party withdrew, and as they escaped this way and that, the Scots became aware of the arrival of the English. They were in a sleepy state at about three o'clock in the afternoon, but immediately roused themselves and flew to arms. At once the Earl of Buchan despatched his kinsman Robert Stewart of Ralston, a man most active as a fighter, with thirty lightly armed archers whose task was to seek out fords or a crossing of the deep stream at Baugé.

As they approached a certain arched and narrow bridge, the Duke of Clarence – Henry V's brother – arrived with banner unfurled seeking to cross the bridge. The said Robert and his men stood their ground opposite him in manly fashion and obstructed his passage until about a hundred Scots belonging to the retinue of Master Hugh Kennedy, who were lodged in a church nearby, arrived and offered major impediment to the passage of the English, until with the greatest of difficulty and furious fighting and leaving their horses behind, the Duke and his men gained a passage across the bridge on foot and sought the open country near Baugé.

The Earl of Buchan collected scarcely two hundred men as front line troops by the sound of his trumpets and attacked him immediately. The Duke of Clarence was wounded in the face by the lance of the Lord of Swinton and met his end after being struck to the ground by the Earl of Buchan's mace. Meanwhile the English rushed together in swarms from all directions; they joined the fight, were wounded and taken prisoner, killed and put to flight well into the deep darkness of the night.

On the side of the Scots no more than twelve fell, and these from among the common soldiers; from among the French gentlemen only two fell, namely Charles le Bouteiller and the brother of the Sire de Fontaines. On the English side the dead were Thomas Duke of Clarence, the Earl of Redesdale, the Lord Ros, Lord Grey of Condor and others totalling 1,617 men! On hearing of the victory, Pope Martin V said: "the Scots are well known as an antidote to the English".

The Scots army in France would see action at Orléans in 1429 where this time a waggon train of provisions for the English was attacked. However the Scots were repulsed with the hero of Baugé, Sir John Stewart of Darnley, killed in the action.

In the same year Hugh Kennedy (who would end up Provost of St Andrews) would have 800 men fighting in the wars of Joan of Arc.

The Alliance would be supported and bound by marriage also ... with Edward Balliol son of King John Balliol marrying Joan, daughter of the French King Charles de Valois. In 1436 Louis the Dauphin of France (would be King Louis XI) married Margaret, daughter to James I of Scotland. In 1536 King James V of Scotland married Magdalen the daughter of King Francis I, and King Francis II would marry Mary Queen of Scots in 1558.

But this alliance cost Scotland dear on two occasions. In 1346 at the time of the battle of

Flodden was a total disaster for Scotland, with King James IV and many of his men being killed in the battle.

Crècy between England and France, Scotland to ease pressure on her ally invaded England. King David II was captured and spent ten years in an English prison.

Again, the Scots invaded in 1513 to divert the English from their invasion of France. A huge army 20,000 strong went over the border into England with James IV after a plea of help from the French queen for assistance. It would end in disaster and defeat at the battle of Flodden, with James killed on the field.

King James V died on 14 December in 1542 leaving a two-week-old daughter and his French wife. Soon an English invasion (later named the "rough wooing") started in Scotland bringing a torrid wave of violence to try to convince the Scots to marry the infant Queen Mary to Henry VIII's son Edward.

While the Regent (Arran) was thinking favourably towards the proposal put to him by King Henry VIII in 1543 – the possible union of marriage between the two infant royals, Mary of Scotland and Edward of England, Cardinal Beaton of St Andrews went mad at the news.

According to historian William Robertson, he "complained loudly that the regent had betrayed the kingdom to its most inveterate enemies, and sacrificed its honour to his own ambition. He foretold the extinction of the true catholic religion under the tyranny of an excommunicated heretic".

But as Arran was thinking it over and the Cardinal was in a furious state, political events turned the matter towards Cardinal Beaton's views and Regent Arran would decide to marry Queen Mary to the Dauphin of France instead.

The Scots merchant navy was continuing its lucrative trade in coal, fish and linen goods towards French ports, but bad weather in the

German sea (North Sea) had put lots of Scottish trading vessels into English ports to shelter from a current storm.

Nothing unusual in this and rents would be paid into English harbourmasters' hands. Both countries were at peace with each other and once the storm abated the crews would exit and be on their way.

Henry VIII thought otherwise. The Scots ships were laden with provisions for the French, the very people England was at war with. He ordered the Scots traders to be jailed and their ships to be seized and condemned, treated as prizes of war.

The Scots thought this a grave insult, and their rage was such the English ambassador could hardly be protected in the city of Edinburgh. Cardinal Beaton with his previous stance against the marriage was now applauded as the defender of the honour and liberty of Scotland.

In the collection of papers belonging to the Duke of Hamilton, Sir Ralf Sadler the English ambassador writes from Edinburgh to London on 1 September 1543: "The stay of the ships has brought the people of this town, both men and women, and especially the merchants, into such a rage and fury, that the whole town is commoved against me, and swear great oaths, that if their ships are not restored ... they will set my house here on fire above my head, so that one of us should not escape alive ... This is the unreasonableness of the people, which live here in such a beastly liberty, that they neither regard God nor governor, nor yet justice, or any good policy, doth take place among them, assuring your highness that, unless the ships be delivered, there will be none abiding here for me without danger."

Four days later he wrote that the rage of the people was so violent that none of his household dared go out of doors, and that the provost of the town had advised him and his people to stay indoors. "They say plainly, I shall never pass out of the town alive, except thay have their ships restored."

On Cardinal Beaton's advice, the queen mother (Mary of Guise) had already agreed to marry Mary to the Dauphin of France. That did not stop Henry VIII continuing to try to get his way.

The English invasion of Scotland in 1544 brought unrelenting violence. A rare account in a book *The History of Scotland in the Reigns of Queen Mary and King James VI*, by William Robertson takes a detailed look at the destruction by the invading English forces...

Towns, towers, steadings, barns, parish
churches, fortified houses ... cast down or
burnt ... 192
Scots slain ... 403
Prisoners taken ... 816
Cattle taken ... 10,386
Sheep ... 12,497
Nags and geldings ... 1,296
Goats ... 200
Bolls of corn ... 850

Another account from 1545 giving the English action between the 8th and the 23rd September with the below burnt and destroyed between Berwick and Roxburgh ...

Monasteries and friaries ... 7
Castles, towers and peels ... 16
Market towns ... 5
Villages ... 243
Mills ... 13
Hospitals (probably travellers' hospices) ... 3

The English army in 1544 consisted of 20,000 men and 6,000 horse with a fleet of up to 200 transports supporting them. While her sergeants organised resistance, Scotland's Queen Mother held out her hand towards the alliance and her home country of France, and they responded by sending Monsieur de Lorges Count of Mountgomery, with 3,500 French auxiliaries landing at Leith and more reinforcements to come. This would start a trench warfare lasting four years around the outskirts of Edinburgh and Broughty with each side committing outrages against the other.

As the wheels of the French war machine turned to help Scotland, masses of French battalions gathered near the ports for inspection and embarkation towards the French fleet. At a village near Nantes the French suffered a blow to their army before they had even left their own country.

"Monsieur d'Andelot, Colonel of the French infantry came to a village called Pellerin near Nantes, where the forces now ready for the voyage, were rendezvousing. As he observed the air of the officers and soldiers, their order, ranks and march, the foot saluted him with a general discharge, which unhappily laid the Chevalier de Bonnivet dead upon the spot. This gentleman, justly esteemed for his valour and wisdom, was heartily lamented by all that knew him. Immediately a diligent search is made through all the regiments, for the author of the fatal shot, and at last a soldier being seized, merely upon suspicion, owned that his piece had been charged with a brace of bullets; the Chevalier was found to have been wounded by both, and the unhappy wretch was hanged in the burial-place of Pellerin."

At Jedburgh in the Scottish Borders the castle was captured by the English, and then assaulted by the Scots and French and taken by force, using tables held up to ward off the archers. The English captain holding the castle had committed heinous crimes. He was described by the soldier and author Jean de Beaugué as "one of the most barbarous wretches in nature" ... "During the time this monster was in Scotland he never eyed a young woman, but he ravished her, nor an old one unfit to satiate his wild desires but he barbarously murdered". Once this captain had surrendered, a Scots man came forward "eying in the person of this tyrant, the ravisher of his wife and daughters, and unable to contain his resentment, came up ere anybody could discover his meaning, and at one blow struck off the wretch's head, so neatly that it fell full four paces from the body".

The Scots were no better in their atrocities. Jean de Beaugué reports... "I remember, they [the Scots] purchased one of the prisoners from myself for a horse; they tied him neck and heels, laid him down in a plain field, run upon him with their

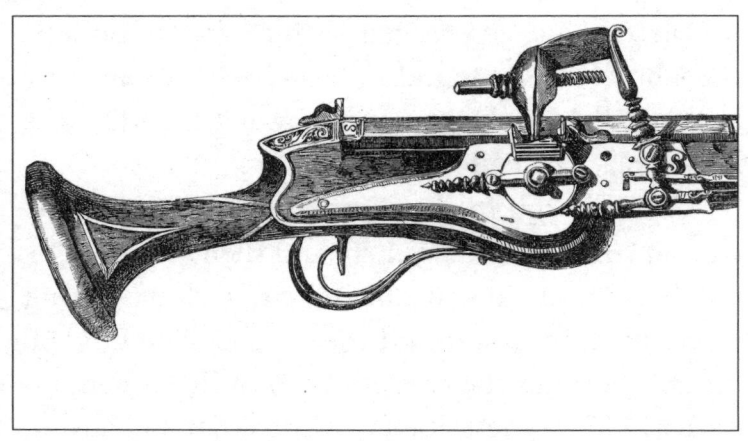

A breech-loading wheel-lock pistol of the sixteenth century.

lances, armed as they were, and on horseback, killed him, cut his body to pieces and carried the divided parcels on the sharp end of their spears. I cannot much commend the Scots for this usage; we had not the same reason to delight in doing ill to our enemy, but the truth is the English had tyrannised over that part of Scotland in the most barbarous manner, and I do not find, that 'twas an injustice to repay them, as the saying is, in their own coin."

Another instance of Scots brutality was noted after a French/Scots successful attack on an English fort emplacement around the Haddington area when trench warfare was ongoing. Jean de Beaugué writes in his diaries: "The Scots thronged to the camp and beheld the naked and mangled bodies of the English stretched out upon the ground, with an air rather of resentment than pity; nay, some, who no doubt had suffered most of their insulting enemy, had the cruelty to pull out the eyes of the dead. So true it is, that men when affected with hatred, must needs be estranged to reason, and I know not after all, whether that hatred which take its rise from the love of one's country, may not rank amongst the number of virtues."

The alliance would carry on right up to Bonnie Prince Charlie's rebellion of 1745. On King Louis' orders, a detachment of men was provided, consisting of men from Irish regiments in the French king's service. Although some of them were captured before landing in Scotland, fifty men on horseback formed the prince's guard and were present at the battle of Culloden. And it was a French ship that ultimately rescued Bonnie Prince Charlie after he went on the run.

Chapter Four

The Rough Wooing 1544–48

At this time in Scotland there was a huge military influence of the French here around the court of Mary of Guise. Mary had been widowed by the death of King James V in 1542; it was the failure of the battle of Solway Moss on 24th November in Cumberland, so it is said, that took him to his bed in a depression from which he never recovered.

Solway Moss came about because, once Henry VIII of England had turned Protestant, he tried to convince James V to do to likewise. A meeting was arranged to discuss the matter in York, but to Henry's anger James never even bothered (or dared) to turn up.

Furious at this, Henry sent an army towards Scotland at which James sent his favourite Oliver Sinclair to meet the threat with 15,000 men. It seems the Scots force had confusion over who was in command. Robert Lord Maxwell who was the Border Marshall should have had control, but the Scots when confronted with the English refused to fight for Oliver. A small skirmish took place with fewer than thirty killed, and then the Scots surrendered. James V was totally humiliated and died from a broken heart!

When he died, his daughter Mary was only six days old. Mary was crowned Queen of Scots, then Regents were chosen to preside over Scotland's interests on her behalf while she was brought up. Although she was a child the Scottish Parliament decided she was to be married to the dauphin, who was heir to the French throne and would go on to be king of France for a short time – King Francis II. But in 1544 an alternative marriage proposal had been offered to the young – two years old – Mary Queen of Scots by the English King Henry VIII. His intention was to stop the potential French marriage (and Scotland staying Catholic in faith) and to unify the crowns of Scotland and England, by marrying Henry's son Edward (later to be Edward VI) to Mary Queen of Scots.

But with St Andrews Chancellor Cardinal Beaton in power, Scotland's nobles thought over the proposal and then refused the offer. They were far too committed to the planned union with

France and resolved to keep Scotland Catholic and away from English and Protestant ambitions.

Henry VIII was not a man to be refused! Furious that the marriage had fallen through, he then sent his warlords Edward Seymour, Earl of Hertford, later known as the Duke of Somerset, and his brother the Lord Admiral Thomas Seymour to force an aggressive hand in the matters (as already mentioned, they both held their positions due to Henry being married to their sister Jane Seymour, who had died in 1537). With Henry VIII so aged and ill at this time (he was to die in January 1547), he had the Earl of Hertford placed as his son's mentor and steward and ordered him to flatten Scottish resistance to the wedding proposal.

Later described as "the rough wooing", it was Henry VIII's mind to smash the defiance of Scotland with its refusal of the wedding in a brash wave of methodical violence. At first a large English cavalry force under Lord Eure was sent against the Scottish border towns in the spring of 1544, destroying the abbeys of Melrose, Jedburgh and Kelso. A massive army soon followed across the border under the guidance of Lord Hertford with 35,000 men at arms in a wave of destruction and burning, heading towards Edinburgh and the

Melrose Abbey as it was in bygone days.

port of Leith. As this mounted force and army of foot soldiers created a wave of destruction in southern Scotland, at sea King Henry's navy under Admiral Thomas Seymour came up the east coast of England shadowing the land forces, with over forty men-o'-war and transport ships to supply the army. Both forces were en route to Leith harbour, where navy and army would meet. The admiral was set to reduce to ashes the proud, productive Scottish harbours along the Fife and East Lothian coastlines as he made towards Leith.

The Scots were utterly unprepared for this sudden violence, or for invasion in such numbers, but they did manage to address the aggression in February 1545, when a hastily gathered force of Scots under James Hamilton attacked a much larger force of English knights and foot soldiers, numbering over 5,000 men, at Ancrum Moor on the Borders and heavily defeated them, killing the leaders Sir Ralph Eure (Lord Eure's son and heir) and Sir Brian Layton. With this unexpected setback, English ambitions were curbed for a while, but they renewed the invasion with further heavy incursions in September 1545 and then again, after Henry VIII's death, in September 1547.

Edinburgh was attacked but put up stout resistance resulting in trench warfare, although a large part of the outskirts was burnt.

According to Thomson's *History of the Scottish People*, "Scarcely a village south of Edinburgh was not destroyed and Craigmillar castle was burned to the ground".

Almost inevitably a confrontation on a grand scale developed with the large English army stationed at Newcastle, under the command of the Earl of Hertford, mobilising 4,000 cavalry and 12,000 men, and then advancing through lower Scotland with a reported 12,000 waggons supporting the army's needs. The light horse were led by eyepatch-wearing Sir Francis Bryan (nicknamed the Vicar of Hell, it is said by Henry VIII himself) and there were 500 Italian mercenaries and another 200 mounted Spanish ones. The army was once more supported from the sea by Admiral Seymour, with command given to Lord Clinton.

Scotland had more than its fair share of traitors at this time, who had secretly promised to help England. According to James Taylor's *Pictorial History of Scotland*, "The most prominent among these most infamous traitors were the Earls of Bothwell, Cassillis and Marischal, Lord Kilmaurs, eldest son of the Earl of Glencairn, Lord Grey, and the notorious Sir George Douglas. Bothwell had promised to transfer his allegiance to the English Government, and to surrender to them his strong castle of Hermitage, on condition that he should receive the hand of the Duchess of Suffolk, aunt to the young English monarch."

The land force slowly worked its way through Cockburnspath, where spies brought news of the Scottish forces. At Dunglass Castle the few occupants were burned out and the castle was reduced to rubble. Next came Innerwick and Thornton Castle, which held out against the English army for a few days before suffering the same fate as Dunglass Castle.

Before the Earl of Douglas's castle at Tantallon the army considered bringing about the demise of the stronghold, but with further news of Scottish forces mobilising against them it was reckoned that the castle might take weeks rather than days to subdue, so to keep the men fresh they advanced towards the outskirts of Edinburgh and Prestongrange, where Fawside Castle was seen as easier fodder. It was soon reduced to ashes, with little resistance. This was where the reckoning would be made with the Scots: the English dug in and with support from the navy in view they felt it was a good position to prepare the army on the high ground.

The Scottish retaliated with a hastily gathered force. A Scottish army under the Regent Arran moved out from Edinburgh to face this English threat.

Regent Arran was James Hamilton, the Earl of Arran and first cousin to James IV. Before Queen Mary had a son, Arran was next in line for the Scottish throne after her.

The battle of Pinkie was fought near Musselburgh in 1547 and victory went to the English forces.

With the two armies facing each other, Arran offered a duel to Somerset!

Twenty men apiece with Somerset and Arran would contest the matter as gentlemen.

But Somerset was not inclined to take up the challenge, declaring: "We have had a good season in this country; and I am here now but with a sober company, and they a great number; and if they would meet us in field they will be satisfied with fighting enough!"

Just south of Musselburgh and Inveresk, both sides prepared for the coming battle; the ground in front was known as as Pinkie Cleugh. The coming battle would end in utter disaster for the Scots; the

English were to win a decisive battle against them at this Pinkie Cleugh on 13th September 1547.

The Scottish army led by Lord Arran and the Earl of Angus positioned the army of around 22,000 pikemen close to the shore monitoring the English host. The English army was now around 18,000 strong with naval support from thirty-two ships sitting off the coast. It was this seaborne assistance that would win the day.

The battle was started by a cavalry charge from the Scots – 1,500 horse under Lord George Home, one of the Scottish nobles, but he was completely outnumbered by the English horse of 4,000. The fight was brisk and the Scots were heavily defeated and lost most of their force when they rode too close to the English trying to taunt them to come down from the high ground. The Scots cavalry wheeled about in front of the English position with their flanks exposed.

The English saw their opportunity and charged into the Scots, catching them completely out of position and unable to turn about and give fight. This engagement was short but fierce with the Scots losing nearly a thousand horses. Lord Home himself was injured when his horse fell, and his own son was captured by the English. He took the remnants of this disaster back to the Scottish

The battle of Pinkie – Lord Grey of Wilton's charge.

lines, but overall in one foolish move the army had lost its cavalry shield.

The English Captain of Horse was William Lord Grey of Wilton. In a memoir of Lord Grey's life, his son described the moment the Scots horse wheeled in front of him, exposing their flank and irresistible to the charge that followed: "Our camp had no sooner taken their march but that the Scots on every side came pricking and huing after their old wont. My lord's men forbore a great while, till at the last 400 or 500 of them coming scattered on the spur with a marvellous shout within their staves' length of the foremost troop, and thinking then, as was their guise, to have wheeled about, Gaynesford, the leader of the troop and lieutenant of my lord's own band, cried the charge, which as hotly as unlooked for being given, from charging in sport the Scots fell to running away in earnest, whereat the rest of their horsemen (esteemed at the fewest 1,000), being amazed, fell likewise to the trying of their horses' speed. Thus was the greatest part of the Scottish force in horsemen this day overthrown, and a great sort of prisoners taken, amongst which the Earl of Huntley was one."

Lord Grey in hot pursuit got a pike wound in the mouth but survived the battle. Although the Scots army was larger than the English in numbers, the quality of fighting men in armour was lacking. English cannon from their high position found the Scottish army in good range, and in unison the thirty ships sitting unopposed off the coastline fired murderous shot at the stationary Scots force. The cannonade was joined by the English land armament with attention now deployed to the Scots front.

The English army advanced and the Scots vanguard was attacked by a wall of thousands of English pikemen as the English fleet now rained down shot among the Scots rearguard, laying

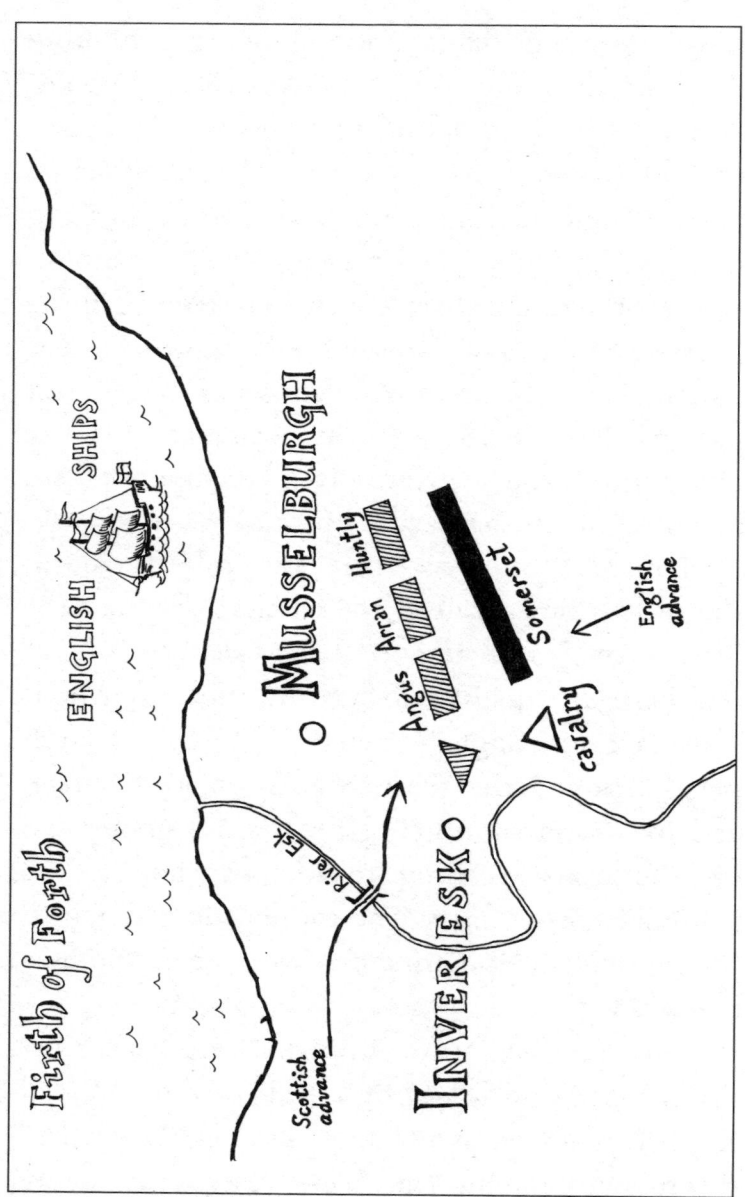

The battle of Pinkie was fought south of Musselburgh.

whole divisions low. This was unsustainable pressure and there was no Scots fleet on the horizon to defend against the invader. It was impossible for the army to suffer such loses and retain any battle formation. The reserve English divisions were mainly archers and they now let loose, with the assault coming from three sides. No relief could be offered from the depleted Scots cavalry.

Hit from sea, forward and flank, the Scots army inevitably collapsed and broke formation, thousands of men fleeing towards Edinburgh as the English now released their cavalry in the chase — 300 horse under Sir John Luttrel. With not enough Scots horse units to hamper the English charge, they cut the Scots down in the confusion. The dead were found all the way to Edinburgh in the chase, numbering maybe 6,000 (some reports put it as high as 14,000). Most of the dead were found with great sabre wounds to the head, killed in flight by the cavalry. (The English found it hard to pick out Scottish nobles from common men, as all had the same leather jerkins. If they could have been identified, the nobles would have been spared for further ransom later on.)

English losses were near 600 dead, and they had lost some of their own nobles unseated from their horses by Scots pikemen. Nevertheless it was a great victory for the English, and the day would be named Black Sunday in Scottish mouths for many a year.

On the battlefield was William Patten, an English government official who oversaw the battle, who would later write a book, *The Expedicion into Scotlande*. In it he describes the aftermath and the terrible sights of the field of Pinkie Cleugh: "A pitiful sight of the dead corpses lying dispersed abroad, some their legs cut off, some but houghed, and left lying half dead, some thrust quite through the body, others the arms cut off, diverse the necks half a sunder, many their heads cloven, of sundry the brains pasht out, some others again their heads quite off, with many other kinds of killing ... for the most part killed either in the head or in the neck, for our horsemen could not well reach lower with their swords ... the river ran all red with blood".

The English army then made a permanent camp in the area of the victory. It was strategically important that they were near the coast of Dunbar and as previous English armies invading into Scotland had found out, the Scots usually burned all before them in a scorched-earth policy when invaded. It was a way of starving the great English army into evasive action: all food resources that could not be rescued were burned by the Scots to prevent the English using them. It was thus important for the English army to be constantly supplied by their navy.

The Scottish queen's half-brother Lord James Stewart was still at large in the field with a small Scottish army near St Andrews, where the previous year the cardinal of St Andrews had been murdered in his own castle.

Cardinal Beaton had been one of the figures who rejected Henry VIII's marriage proposal. He had recently, against public opinion, condemned the protestant reformer George Wishart as a heretic. His judgement was for George to be burnt at the stake outside St Andrews Castle*. In response to this act the Protestant reformers across Fife including some soon to be big players in Scottish history, Kirkcaldy of Grange, John Melville and John Knox, plotted the cardinal's downfall.

* NOTE: When George was being burned Cardinal Beaton and his bishops sat in soft cushions upon the castle walls, eating and drinking wine while enjoying the entertainment. Unknown to them, George Wishart's supporters had fastened large bags of gunpowder about his waist under his shirts to hasten his death. The gunpowder blew up, damaging Wishart's legs, but also blowing several of the cardinal's men off the castle roof (one died).

In October 1546 the Fife Protestants, friends and supporters of George Wishart's teachings, had surprised the cardinal's castle at dawn: there were some rebuilding works taking place at the castle and the assassins posed as builders to gain entry to the castle. Once across the drawbridge a small number of them searched the corridors looking for Beaton. They broke into the cardinal's own bedchamber and ran him through the body with a claymore sword as he begged for mercy, dressed in nothing but his bedclothes.

The attackers took the castle and held it. They were all Protestants rebelling against Catholic rule in Scotland. The town guard outside wanted proof the cardinal was actually dead and the reformers tied a bed sheet around the arm and leg of Cardinal Beaton and hung the naked body for all to see out the castle window. By Robert Lyndesay's account, "In this manner he hung while one of his murderers, a man called Guthery, pissed into his mouth!" A gory sight for sure, but the message had been sent!

The then Regent Arran, James Hamilton, attacked the castle but only half-heartedly (his son was captive inside). As months went past a French fleet arrived with armed forces to help take the castle from the Protestants inside (France was

Engraving of the ruins of St Andrews Castle.

allied to Scotland and Queen Mary, only five years old at the time, was due to marry the king of France). The siege lasted a year till 30th July 1547 when the castle was eventually blown apart by French cannon that had been lifted high up to the cathedral tower called "Rules Tower". From this 33-metre-high elevated position, the cannon tore the castle walls apart. The defenders, now with no means to defend themselves, surrendered to the French and were taken as prisoners back to France in their ships. The French ransacked the castle, taking as booty all the silver and gold relics it had (supposedly over £100,000 Scots, all the cardinal's loot). It was just two months later that the English would crush the Scots army at the battle of Pinkie Cleugh.

The River Tyne in Haddington.

With Regent Arran's forces now scattered, it was now seen as too dangerous for Mary in Scotland. She was to be sent to France for her own safety as hostilities continued. With the castle subdued, the naval power that had reduced the castle of St Andrews now returned to France. But there would still have been a considerable force of French soldiery left in the area and with Scots resistance against the English springing up everywhere they were kept busy. At this time the English host in Haddington was being monitored carefully for its next move. The English camp decided to spoil the country around them further in an orgy of violence and plunder, to force the Scots to a further showdown.

English ships had sailed north to attack Scotland. Fascinating records survive, including instructions to Andrew Dudley, appointing him Admiral of the fleet in 1547 and ordering him to take seven ships north, making it clear that he was to engage any Scots he encountered. The instructions mention a Scottish fleet ("28 sail of Scots"). Dudley was also instructed to show himself off St Andrews sometimes to frighten the Scottish enemies of England and comfort England's friends there.

The English looked with eager eyes to the Fife coastline. With licence from their admiral, the fleet set sail. Across the water to Fife from Haddington the grand fleet came. Planning to pillage and destroy as they had done in the border towns, they looked to the sea ports of Anstruther and Pittenweem where there was ample space to berth their galleons of war and land their ground troops. But when they came within range of the Scots coastal harbours they found them bristling with cannons and armed men ready for defiant action. The English fleet in the Firth of Forth, now under the command of Lord Clinton, was not ready to risk a confrontation against these coastal defences. They did see an easier prize: the relatively undefended harbour of St Monans. A

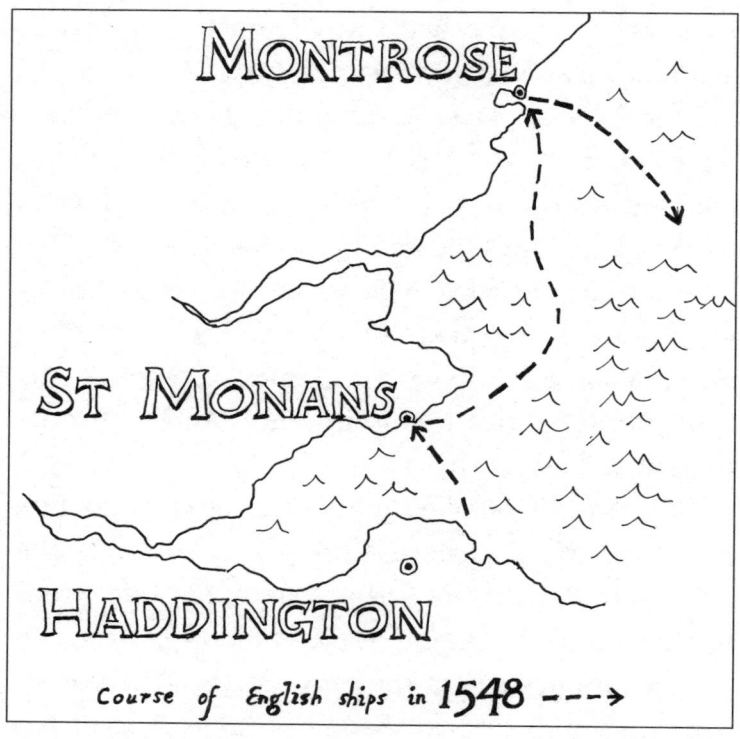

Course of English ships in 1548 ---->

Map showing the route from East Lothian to Fife and beyond.

landing could be easily made there on the carse stone beach, and from there the town of St Andrews, which is just twelve kilometres away, could be assaulted from behind. Many farms could be raided for supplies along the way.

The Scottish forces were in Edinburgh defending the trenches with their French allies. Fife must have looked a very soft target indeed, and very inviting to the admiral ... what a mistake!

Chapter Five

The Attack

The English captains in 1548 knew St Monans well. In the year 1544 the Fife harbours along this coastline were put under fierce cannonade from the English fleet in the first wave of the "rough wooing". St Monans harbour was attacked by an English sea force under the command of Captain Nicholas Poyntz, who had already attacked and damaged the harbours of Kinghorn, Queensferry and Burntisland.

When the fleet reached St Monans, Nicholas on board a mighty galleon called the *Great Galley* fired on the harbour with heavy cannon. He destroyed and sank the entire fishing fleet there, which was undefended, ruining the harbour, and then turned the guns on the abbey building, knocking great holes in the masonry. The Benedictine monks living there stood helpless as the cannons did their damage, eventually setting the place ablaze. The monastery, although being extensively damaged from the English attack, was repaired over the next two years.

At the time of the "rough wooing", the harbours along this coastline were relatively undefended and offered easy practice for the English gunners. The damage to the fishing fleet would have had an enormous impact in this community, with Pittenweem the twelfth richest area of Scotland at that time*. The locals realised that preparations had to be made for this area's protection, because a further attack of the same scale was always possible while the English were still in a hostile mood. Any such attack would have to be thwarted.

By 1548 the Fife lairds were better prepared for the return of the English invader. To organize their defence they had gathered a force about them, and were ready to make a reckoning for the previous hurt the invader had done to this coastline. The two lairds of Largo, Andrew and John Wood, came from a family famed in the wars with England: they were the sons of the great admiral and defender of Scotland, Sir Andrew Wood (died 1540)**, who had destroyed the

* NOTE: According to records in David Cook's *Annals of Pittenweem* 1840.
** NOTE: For more information on this great sea warrior, see my book *Largo's Untold Stories*.

English in three major sea battles in the Forth during the reigns of James III and IV.

An early warning system was devised, with huge fires set along the Fife coast on the hills of Elie and the 300-metre-high Largo Law.

Once signs of invasion were afoot, these great beacons of fire were lit and the lairds of Largo and others knew the English were coming. They looked eastwards towards the sea and saw the sails of the English warships. The Scots forces, resolute in defence of their homeland, prepared themselves, armed in boiled leathers, mail and plate, and made haste towards St Monans – the direction in which the English host seemed to be heading.

The English under their great Admiral Lord Seymour, who was sick of the land forces gaining all the glory, decided to attack Fife directly across from the base at Haddington. Seymour had his captain Lord Clinton commanded to sail the two dozen warships, one galleon and thirty other transports from off the Dunbar coast, intending to land a great number of their troops unopposed in Fife at the village of St Monans in the shadow of Newark Castle, home of Sir James Sandilands.

From here he could rampage across the land at will, and as St Andrews was now free from the French castle besiegers, it should have been

The environs of Newark Castle.

relatively easy to plunder. It is possible that was his target: to capture St Andrews, the biggest religious stronghold in Scotland, which was apparently there for the taking ... that would have put the name Seymour in high standing.

A multitude of flat-bottomed marine transports offloaded at least 1,200 soldiers on to the beach (five thousand in some accounts). On the beachhead, as the English army disembarked, they observed movement along the clifftop. They could see an unorganised group of lightly armed men: this would probably be Sir James Sandilands arming what few trained soldiers he had and trying to organise his peasant workers and fishermen as best he could in preparation of some attempt at defence.

The English, in observing the Scots on the clifftops, set up some small ordnance cannons straight from the ships and fired some shot up at the group, which immediately dispersed them. But the other Fife lords were not idle. The lairds

The rocky foreshore where the English soldiers landed.

of Largo were approaching at speed from the east from their castle estate, with a small armed retainer, and the thunder of the English cannonade in the distance would make it evident that Sandilands' men had made contact. The Largo lairds' men then joined the steel of Sir John Wemyss, who had anticipated the landing and had made secret preparations. Meanwhile Sir James Sandilands' tiny force could do little to prevent the English force moving off the beach, and in the smoke of the cannonade they retreated from the heights overlooking the English landing.

The castle and home of Sir James Sandilands must have been the English army's first prize of the day, and it was taken as Sandilands retreated into the woodland, where he mustered every man available to him from around the farms and villages of St Monans and Abercrombie. Arming his fishermen, millers and peasants with woodaxes and pitchforks to defend their village, it was a motley crew of scared men he scraped together to fight. It must have seemed almost futile, given the thousands they had seen coming off the ships on the beach, but then women and boys joined the number too. The St Monans women had decided they would not stand idle as their menfolk fought and died for them. As they gathered such arms as

Another photo of the remains of Newark Castle, which in 1548 was the home of Sir James Sandilands.

they had, they heard the reports of cannon fire, this time to the west, where another host had arrived! This time a Scots force.

From the north came a better equipped formation, the Prior of St Andrews himself, Lord James Stewart, the Queen's half-brother, and with him what military might he could muster that remained after the recent castle siege. He rode flying the cross of St Andrew with a larger battalion (some of this number, I imagine, would be French soldiers) of well-armed Scots, battle-hardy from the year-long fight to take St Andrews castle. Possibly up to 1,000 men of various fighting quality.

The English fleet had sailed 25 kilometres straight across to the Fife coast landing at St Monans. Below Newark Castle the English were busy on the beach, offloading horses from their flat-bottomed transport ships and setting up a vanguard. Then in the distance war horns sounded, breaking the peace of the remarkably dark dawn! Scouts came into camp reporting movement from the north, and in the distance banners were seen, flying the cross of Scotland. They had not been aware of it, but the minute the English had set foot on St Monans beach, they had walked into a trap! The scouts of Sir John Wemyss had secretly been monitoring the English since their fleet had been spotted at sea. When the English fleet's destination was finally understood, Sir John mobilised his small mobile force towards St Monans, gathering what strength he could from other lairds as he made towards the location of the landing. Preparations to contain the beach landing had been undertaken, with deep trenches dug and filled up with flammable items (tar, straw, bracken and gunpowder) along the grass beachhead.

Pictures of the area where Sir John Wemyss and his forces lay in waiting.

Sir John Wemyss at least had thought out a plan. Sir John gathered his small force and was joined by the Largo lairds Alexander and John Wood, who had also turned out their castle garrison with what quality steel they possessed, strapping on their father's old armour plate. It is reported Sir John Wemyss had only 120 of his own men with him, men who hid in the shallows of the field and forest overnight, monitoring the English landing as they secretly dug the deep trenches. This area of Fife had lost a lot of men due to the recent disaster of the battle of Pinkie and the ongoing war in Edinburgh. It cannot now be accurately estimated what numbers were available to be brought to the field of battle, or what was the quality of the men. But the Largo contingent would have included veteran sailors who had seen action with John and Alexander's father Sir Andrew Wood against the English. Although getting on in years they would still be a force to reckon with.

With the commander on the beach now aware of movement to the north, the English marines and soldiers started to form up into divisions ready to march at first light. With scouts reporting the glint of steel breastplates and armour in the distance, the English now knew they had a fight on their hands with quality opposition. It was Lord James Stewart's contingent, arriving hotfoot from St Andrews. Sir John Wemyss, who had lain all night with his men hidden from sight, now opened up the battle with the first aggressive move, making a raucous noise and a feint with his hidden archers to attract the English off the beach and direct their attentions away from Lord James Stewart. The English men at first fell under an unexpected hail of arrows from the eastern quarter, but they gathered their strength and returned fire. Now it was the Scots who fell under these masters of the yew bow. The initial effect was only to draw the English closer; under the arrows the Scots retreated behind the trench they had dug.

The English took the bait that Sir John Wemyss offered, and charged hard at the Scots position on the clifftop on the west shoreline. At this point both sets of archers were still trading blows ... the deep trenches the Scots had laboured so secretly to dig overnight were then set on fire, creating a thick wave of smoke shielding the Scots numbers from view. In this confusion of thick smoke, three small ordinances were quickly loaded and wheeled forward and primed and readied pointing towards the charging English.

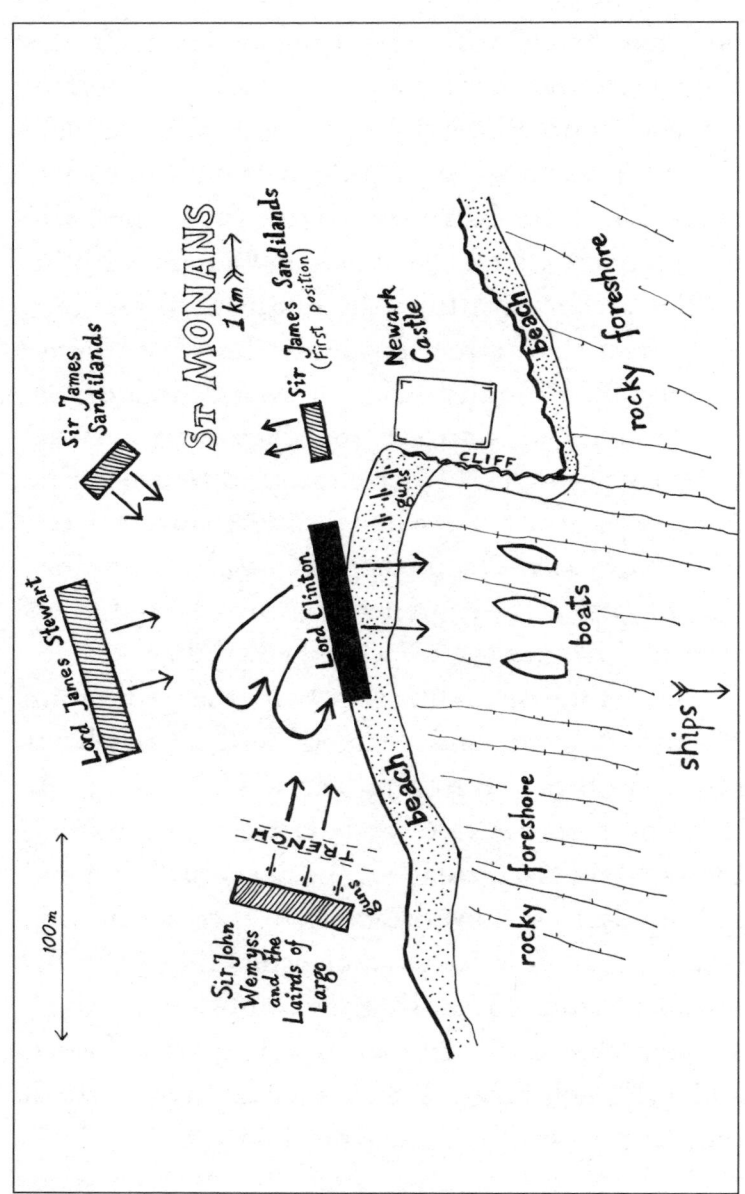

Map of the battle of St Monans, 19 June 1548.

The Scots, and their crouching pikemen, and their best men clad in armour were completely hidden by the smoke. The English fast approached the trench, a mix of steel-clad men and marines shouting out their slogans and their king's name ... as the English reached the trench which had obstructed their view with the reeking smoke, they shielded their eyes and led blind with pike and sword. The Laird of Wemyss gave his signal – and the three cannons, still hidden by the smoke, laden with grapeshot (nails and small lead balls), fired straight into the mass of Englishmen, blasting them into oblivion at pointblank range! The effect was devastating; the English front was shattered; pieces of what had once been men now lay torn asunder!

Arms, legs and heads lay scattered about. Horses were screaming on the field of gore, where men in armour lay helpless, bleeding out to die where they lay. But there were still many divisions of English in the field, coming to take the place of the dead and dying. Wemyss and the Largo lairds now with a great shout threw their steel and armed men forward through the smoke, leaping over the burning trench, and clashed head-on with the oncoming English. Now James Stewart, the queen's half brother, who was only seventeen years

Newark Castle showing where fighting took place.

old, bravely led the main assault on horseback in a suit of armour and with sword drawn, as his men arrived in numbers from St Andrews and charged straight on to the field of battle. Working in a pincer movement, his men cut their way through the English lines to be held on the beachhead as the two forces met in tough hand-to-hand fighting.

The lairds of Largo, as the English front was held in check by Lord Stewart's men, then attacked the English flank with what cavalry they had, in support of Sir John Wemyss' men. More help now came from the local barons of Balcarras and Sir

James Sandilands' men. Angry at the hurt the English had done previously to this town, they now at last had the enemy in front of them to face their fury and their pitchforks and boathooks. The English on the beachhead were in utter confusion, hit from three sides. The cries from the dying and the clash of arms with smoke swirling around gave no indication of how the fight was faring. The English divisions and marines on the rocky beach could not go forward because of the mass of men in the way.

As the English on the beach looked up to the cliff heights they could make out the movements of the women and boys of St Monans. They lost all heart for battle, mistaking the women and children for another army of additional Scots reinforcements coming into the field of battle. As the English on the beach hesitated, they saw numbers of screaming wounded coming down from the beachhead, and before any grouping of reinforcements could be organized, Scottish soldiers were seen streaming down from the hill to get among them. The Englishmen were seasoned soldiers, many from the Pinkie battlefield, but with the crush of bodies and the Scots streaming in numbers from the high ground, experience counted for nothing.

The English were being driven back forcefully! Pikes, war hammers, axes and the steel of swords smote down hard, one blow enough to cut a man from helmet to sternum. Men screaming were pinioned by spears and pikes. Confidence turned to confusion as the English were forced back upon the boats they had arrived in. The fury of the attack completely surprised the English, and the end came suddenly. The English could see no way forward off the beach and so, at first in ones and twos, they tried to get back to the safety of the grand galleons. Then it turned into a rout; this manoeuvre now made them more vulnerable as they turned their backs on the Scots, with hundreds of men now fighting through the sea to get back on board.

W. Patten was serving with the English armed forces and observed military action in person. He covered the struggle in the trench warfare that broke out in the siege of Edinburgh between Scots and French and English and Spaniards over the next two years. His position is mentioned as the Conjoint Judge Marshall. He describes the Scottish war machine in action:

"Hackbutters [soldiers armed with 'hackbuts' or matchlock firearms] have they few or none, and appoint their fight most commonly always a foot.

They come to the field well furnished all with jack [sleeveless tunic] and skull [skullcap], dagger, buckler [small, round shield], and swords all notably broad and thin, of exceeding good temper and universally made to slice, that as I never saw none so good, so think it hard to devise the better: hereto every man his pike and a great kercher [kerchief] wrapped twice or thrice about his neck, not for cold but for cutting. In their array toward the joining with the enemy, they cling and thrust so near in the forerank shoulder to shoulder together, with their pikes in both hands straight afore them, and their followers in that order so hard at their backs, laying their pikes over their foregoers' shoulders, that if they so assail undissevered, no force can well withstand them. Standing at defence, they thrust shoulders likewise so nigh together, the foreranks well nigh to kneeling, stoop low before for their fellows behind, holding their pikes in both hands, and therewith in their left their bucklers, the one end of the pike against their right foot, the other against the enemy breast high, their followers crossing their pike points with them forward, and thus with each other so nigh as place and space will suffer, through the whole ward so thick, that as easily shall a bare finger pierce through the skin of an angry hedgehog, as any encounter the front of their pikes."

The beach became a scene of slaughter. The main Scottish force would have been cavalry, used to reach the area at speed. Here the balance and advantage would be with the Scots. The English transports would have landed cavalry, but in this clash their use could not be exploited – simply because of the mass of men in the way. The beach was now littered by severed limbs and bodies with split skulls. Horsemen were slashing down on running foes as the English tried to disengage from the hellish situation as more Scots appeared on the beachhead. It seemed every downward stroke took another man's life; many were drowned in the flight to the galleons as now helpless they were cut down by sword, pike and pitchfork. Only a few hundred are reported (in many of the accounts) to have made it to the ships, and to relative safety.

But in the confusion of the retreat one ship was overcrowded with desperate men pulling at its sides to get aboard and away from the killing field. When its sails caught the wind, it turned out of control and crashed lopsided into rocks, was overturned and sank with great loss of men. (Wemyss' men, I imagine, may now have turned

Coastline where some of the English soldiers re-embarked.

the three cannons they had at their disposal on to the retreating English ships.)

What had once been proud regiments were now reduced to survivors fighting amongst themselves to get back on board ship – anywhere away from this nightmare beach of slaughter. But the dead and dying left on land and lying floating in the sea in such a small area must have been a sight! In one report it is stated: "Lord Clinton was lucky himself to get back aboard his own ship of command."

The English admiral was now well beaten and with the land forces gridlocked in a stalemate of trenches between the English and French/Scots at Edinburgh, the Scottish courts could act on the many traitors who had helped in various ways the invaders from England. The punishments were severe ... from my first-edition copy of Robert Pitcairn's *Trials in Scotland* Vol I 1488–1568, we have a steady flow of traitors coming to justice in the Scottish courts. As we see, Haddington, from where the troops set off to attack St Monans, had its fair share of traitors.

INTERCOMMUNING WITH THE ENGLISH AT BROUGHTY

Nov 26 1549 – Mr James Betoune denounced rebel, and put to the horn [proclaimed an outlaw], &c. for not underlying the law, for treasonably going to the Fortalice [small fort] of Bruchty, kept by our ancient enemies the English; And for Intercommuning, speaking and treating with Sir John Luterale, Captain thereof, for the subversion and subjugation of the whole country adjoining the said Fortalice; Committed in the months of June, July, August 1548.

SUPPLYING THE ENGLISH AT LAUDER

July 18th 1550 – William Lauder, in Lauder, Convicted of the treasonable Intercommuning, resett [shelter or protection], supply and assistance given to our ancient enemies the English, being within the Fortalice near to the burgh of Lauder; continually furnishing them with meat and drink, from the time of the building thereof, in the month of ... 1547: And for leading and conducting the said English to the foresaid Fortalice, and other places at their will, to the spoiling, wasting, and destruction of the kingdom, and conquest thereof; revealing and shewing to our said enemies the secrets of the kingdom: And specially, for carrying and sending letters and close writings of Sir Hugh Willeby, and other Englishmen, within England and Scotland, in a treasonable manner: And for common treason. – Beheaded.

INTERCOMMUNING WITH THE ENGLISH IN HADINGTON

August 8th 1550 – George Hepburne, in Athelstanefurd, got the Queen's Remission for treasonably Intercommuning with Sir James Wolfurd, General of Hadingtoune, and other Englishmen with him in Hadingtoune, in June 1548, and continually from that time until the expulsion of the Englishmen therefrom; supplying them with sheep, oxen, and victual, and thus plainly participating with and assisting them, and enabling the said Englishmen to hold out the said town longer against the Queen and the lord Governor, to the subversion and destruction of the kingdom. And also, for treasonably dwelling under assurance with the said Englishmen for the foresaid space. — John, James, and Adam Bagbie in Athelstanefurd, were likewise denounced Rebels for the said crime; and Patrick Hepburne of Wauchtoune, their cautioner, was amerciated [fined] for their non-appearance.

Chapter Six

The Letters and Histories

The scarce material I have gathered from letters and French reports on the battle state ...

Lord Herris' memoirs which were gathered and published in 1836 under the title *History of the Reign of Mary Queen of Scots*.

I will write it as it was published in old Scots tongue, except that I have used the modern letter 's' throughout.

"An English Navie by this tyme was come in light of our Scots coasts which terrified the whole cuntrie. They resolve to attempt upon Fyffe, and lands twelve hundred men at a village called S. Minianus. Lord James Stewart the Queen's base brother (who was newlie returned from France), conveens the cuntry about S. Androes, fights the English; and with the loss of six hundred of there men, and one hundred prisoners, he beats them back to there ships. From hence they saill about

the coast, and interprysed something upon
Montros; but by the valor and conduct of the Laird
of Drum, then provost of Montros, there camp was
surprysed in the night, five hundred and more
were killed, and the rest fled to their ships."

The abridgement in the Advocates Library reports
800 invaders killed in the action at St Monans.

The English writer Hollinshead gives an English
account of the action: "The lord admiral
perceiving no likelihood of battle by land, took
upon him to achieve some other enterprises, and
coming to Burntisland, set certain ships on fire
there, of the chiefest in the river; and saluting the
town of Leith as he passed by with cannon shot, he
determined to land some of his men on the north
side of the Forth, to make some spoil within the
country of Fife. But John Erskine, laird of Dun, as
then somewhat diseased, and returned home from
the camp, caused such daily and nightly watch and
ward to be kept, that this enterprise could not be
so secretly conveyed by the Englishmen, but that
the same was perceived, and so prevented, that
upon their landing they were forced to retire with
loss: and happy was he that might first get again
to shipboard.

"For James Stewart, brother to the Queen (hearing of this tumult) came thither in haste with the common people of St Andrews, and some other few citizens which were remaining in the town, to whom the neighbours did also join themselves, understanding the cause of that assembly. The English being now come on land, about 1,200, stood in warlike sort ready for battle, and with fear of the artillery (which they discharged out of their ships) did easily cause the rude multitude to flee away. But this James Stewart (by little and little suppressing the fear of such as fled) did (with such violence) rush upon his enemies, that forthwith he overthrew them, put them to flight, compelled them to return to the sea with great slaughter, when also many of them (as they fled to their ships) were drowned, besides three hundred that were slain, and one hundred taken."

We can see there is some confusion in these accounts, as Erskine of Dun was at Montrose, not in Fife. Robert Lyndesay of Pitscottie, in his *History of Scotland 1436-1565*, tells us of two English attacks. The first happened at Tayport (known in those days as East Ferry or Partincraig):

"Their ships also lay all that year in Taymouth, betwixt Broughty and Dundee; so that the gentlemen of Fife were constrained to watch and ward continually, for safety of their goods. At length, the gentlemen of the country, being advertised that the English had compacted with sundry Scots, to land, by their conduct, at the East-Ferry, and to burn the same, and Leuchars, with the country adjacent, and to be conducted by them safely back to their ships; Lord James Prior of St Andrews, George Earl of Rothes, John Lord of Lindsay, Andrew Wood of Largo, and divers other gentlemen, with the provost and burgesses of St Andrews, came secretly at the break of day, and lay in ambush near to Partincrag, till the English were landed, and began to forage the country. Then they broke forth betwixt them and their ships, and slew to the number of eight score of their best men of war and mariners; of whom they had great missing thereafter in guiding of their ships; so that they had no great desire thereafter to land in Fife."

Nevertheless, a few pages later he writes:

"These Englishmen had victualled Haddington, and, having thus shown themselves, came to Aberlady, and shipped in some of their ablest gentlemen to pass over and spoil the coast of Fife. They came first to Anstruther and Pittenweem, but fearing to land there, these towns being so populous, they came well against St Ninians, where they landed, thinking to march on foot at Pittenweem, and fortify the same with men and victuals, and to spoil the country. As they were coming to St Ninians-Muir in arrayed battle, with some artillery brought from their ships, Lord James commendator of St Andrews, the lairds of Wemyss and Largo, with sundry others of the country, when they saw the fires arising, came posting thither, and joining with the common people who had convened to stop the landing, skirmished so hotly with them, that they chased them back to their ships, and slew a great number of them, beside many that were drowned and taken captives. There died to the number of six hundred and twelve, and a hundred prisoners taken. This befell in June, in the year foresaid."

(Robert Lyndesay, tenant of Pitscottie, near Ceres in Fife, was alive at the time of the battle.)

Calderwood in his *The History of the Kirk of Scotland* writes...

"The English fleets went about to land their souldiours at Sanct Minnans, in Fife, but the queen's brother, James Stewart, encountered them with speed, and compelled them to retire, after they had landed about twelve hundreth. Three hundreth were slaine, ane hundreth taken, manie drowned."

John Lesley, Bishop of Ross.

Bishop Lesley (John Lesley, Bishop of Ross 1527–96) gives the most complete details of the action...

"It happened so that the laird of Wemyss, that same night the admiral purposed to come to land, came down himself to search the watch before day; and perceiving the light which the Englishmen had in their ships, as then wished to set their men on land, whereupon doubting the worst (a thing that seldom brings repentance), with all diligence he ... went down to the place where he had seen the light, two miles off from the town of St Monans, to understand what the matter might mean; and ... he came so near to the enemies, that he both heard and saw their manner as well as he could wish to do ... in the break of day, they were received at the first shot of arrows, and handled for a while with skirmishes right sharply ... at length the Scottish men retired within certain trenches, where they kindled certain ferns, straw and other things prepared for the purpose, and made a marvellous great smoke and fell back; and there they had three pieces of small artillery, which they discharged so directly ... that no small number of Englishmen were slain; while the laird of Wemyss with that company which he had with him in the trenches, set upon the enemy's front with a great furious noise, dinging them down in heaps; but also another company ... behind the back of a hill began to show themselves, making such a hideous noise and cry as though they would have borne down all before them; and yet that band was but of the meaner sort of people, principally women and children, least able to work any great feat ... The Englishmen not perceiving the fraud, took them to their heels and fled toward their ships, scattered here and there without order; whom the Scottish followed in close, even hard to the water side, and slew divers of them within the water ere they might recover their boats. Of one thousand that came on land, there returned not three hundred to their ships, but was either drowned or slain. The admiral himself hardly escaped to his ship, commanded the sails to be hoisted up, and so departed ..."

This version is slightly abridged and put into more modern English. The description is recorded in full towards the end of this book, as it was written in old Scots.

The Scots historian George Buchanan in his book, *History of Scotland* (originally written in Latin and published the year after his death, in 1582), describes the battle ...

"The whole weight of the war by land, being directed towards Haddington, the leaders of the enemy, thinking that the neighbouring counties must be defenceless, determined to make a descent on the coast of Fife. Wherefore, having sailed past several well inhabited maritime villages, they landed at the populous village of St Minians, whence they might march by land to larger, but less fortified places, of which the spoil would better reward their exertions. James Stewart, the queen's brother, on the first alarm hastened hither with the people of St Andrews, and a number of the countrymen who had been left at home, and was joined in his progress by many in the vicinity. The English, who were already landed, about twelve hundred strong, stood drawn up in order of battle, and by the terror of their cannon, which they brought from the vessels, easily dispersed a crowd of rustics. James, however, having rallied the fugitives, rushed upon the enemy with such impetuosity, that although the greater part of his followers were a hastily collected crowd, he instantly attacked, routed, and chased them to the sea, with great slaughter. Many fell in the fight, and not a few were drowned in the hurry of re-embarking. One boat, with all on board, sunk, in the confusion of putting off to the vessels. On that day, six hundred were said to be killed, and one hundred taken prisoners."

Sir James Balfour gives a short account in his book, *Annales of Scotland*. It was written in 1630 but published in 1824 as James Balfour, *Historical Works* Vol I.

"But the Lord Clinton, riding at anchor with his ships, lands some 5,000 men on the coast of Fife, to spoile the country; but before they did much harm, they were rencountered by the Laird of Wemyss, and the Barons of Fife, all well horsed, who rode them flat down with their horses; and having killed above 700 of them, forced the remnant to save themselves by wading in sea to the necks, before they could gain their flat bottomed boats. Having purched [obtained] no better booty there than their back full of strokes and wet skins, the good entertainment the English did receive in Fife at this time, saved it in all the progress of this war from any further trouble."

Some other historians are quoted in George L. Craik's *Pictorial History of England*:

"According to Burnet, who makes the admiral of the fleet to have been the Protector's brother, Lord Seymour of Sudley, the descent on the Fife coast was made at St Minins (or St Monance), where twelve hundred of the English, after having brought their cannon to land, were repulsed by the country people, headed by James Stuart, Prior of St Andrews, afterwards the celebrated regent Moray, six hundred being slain, and a hundred taken prisoners. They afterwards made a descent during the night at Montrose, where in like manner they were driven off by the peasantry, headed by Erskine of Dun; of eight hundred who had landed, scarcely one in three getting back safe to the ships. 'So,' it is added, 'the admiral got nothing but loss and disgrace by the expedition.'"

There is an interesting mention in the Wemyss family history of a vessel sunk near St Monans: "It is probably more than a mere coincidence that a pinnace, which was sunk at St Monans about the time of this engagement, was, when recovered, gifted by Patrick, Earl of Bothwell, admiral of Scotland, with all its artillery and fittings, to the laird of Wemyss."

The original documentation is published under a heading that says that Patrick Earl Bothwell, Admiral of Scotland, presented a pinnace wrecked at St. Monance to John Wemyss of that Ilk on 8th June 1549. In old Scots, it details the pinnace. I have used more modern spelling, to make it understandable: "ane pinnace, which was drownit at Saint Monans, in the month of September last bypast, now pertaining to us by reason of escheat [confiscation] through right and privilege of admiralty ... Which pinnace perishit at Saint Monans, and afterward was recoverit and relievit, and now is in the hands and possession of Maister Johnne Arnot, Thomas Adesoun, Alexander Adesoun, and certain others partners of them: to be held and to be had, the said pinnace, with all artillery and goods which was within the same the time of her perishing aforesaid, to the said Johnne Wemys of that ilk".

From what I can find on a pinnace boat* it appears that at that time it was a small light vessel, usually two-masted and schooner-rigged, often used as a tender or a scout.

Smarting from this defeat, the English survivors sailed the battered fleet around the Fife coast and headed northwards. Meeting harbours with cannons pointed their way and hostile to their intentions, they stayed to the coastline till the morning of 20th June 1548. Presumably the town of Montrose looked like the place to land and finally get some plunder. Without any defences it looked easy for attack. The English commanders had learned nothing from the St Monans shambles.

Although they were hoping to land unopposed, the Provost of Montrose John Erskine had been rather busy. The English command had just made another big mistake!

John Erskine of Dun was born in Angus in 1509. He was the first-born from the ancient and honourable barons of that country. He was Provost and high constable of Montrose, where his grandfather had held the position before him. It was his duty to provide the defence of Montrose.

---

* NOTE: According to *Tudor Sea Power*, by David Childs, a pinnace style ship is mentioned in the Admiralty of England records, as missing in 1548; called the Black Pinnace, it was 80 tonnes and carried 17 guns.

From the biography of Erskine of Dun by 'Scoto-Britannico' (published 1879) we get an insight into the battle.

"Erskine of Dun, as Provost of Montrose and High Constable, offices which his grandfather had held before him, had to provide for the defence of the town against any hostile descent. A night attack was attempted by the English fleet, but the inhabitants had warning of their approach. Calderwood's account of the affair is as follows:—

"'They thought to have surprised Monrose; but by the vigilance of Johne Areskine, Laird of Dun, Proveist of the toun, their interprise was perceaved and prevented, and they driven backe to their shippes with the losse of some men.'

"The English fleet came hither expecting no opposition, and by this time he had encouraged so plentifully that a thousand men were in arms, and placed sentinels in every part where they were most likely to be attacked; and he selected three hundred men to be shrouded until he gave them the signal. By the break of day the fleet hastened to the town, and were quite unprepared for a defeat. The Laird of Dun managed so skilfully as to force on the retreat of the enemy. They never looked back at the pursuing Scots, but at length gained their ships, much the worse for their encounter."

More detail is given in Buchanan's history:

"Thence the fleet sailed to the Mearns, a less populous district, with the intention of surprising Montrose, a town situate not far from the mouth of the river Dee. They resolved to make their descent during the night, and remained at anchor, without sight of land, till the light departed; but when they approached the shore in the dark, they betrayed their secret design to the enemy, by their own imprudence in hoisting lights on all their boats. John Erskine of Dun, the provost of the town, ordered all the inhabitants to take arms without noise, and divided them into three bands. Some he placed at the back of a sand bank, raised to prevent the landing of the enemy. He himself led the dart-men and other light armed troops, against the invader. The third band, consisting of servants, and a promiscuous crowd of the common people, with a few military men to direct them, he ordered to wait behind the nearest sand hill. Having thus arranged his preparations, he proceeded with his party, and briskly attacked the enemy as they were landing, and in an irregular skirmish drew them towards the sand hill. There, forming a junction with the other party, who were drawn up in order of battle, they all attacked the enemy, who, notwithstanding, did not give way, till the others on the neighbouring hill showed themselves with their banners; then, at last, they ran with such haste to the sea and to their ships, that of about eight hundred who landed, scarcely a third part escaped."

Jean de Beaugué was a French soldier serving Scotland in the wars of 1544–48. In his book, when he wrote about the Scottish defence against England at the battle of Montrose he stated that "of 900 not 100 got again to their ships".

Lord Dun's services in defence of the realm were rated by the full value of his heroic efforts. 'Scoto-Britannico' tells us that in the Dun charter chest there are three letters from Mary of Guise (James V's wife). She speaks of ... "your gude service done to our dearest dochter your soverane".

After the defeat at Montrose, Lord Seymour, the High Admiral "was obliged with heavy loss and disgrace to return to England" (according to Rev Thomas Thomson's *A History of the Scottish People*, Volume 3, 1895).

I have already mentioned a book in my library called *History of St Monance* (written in 1844) by a resident from the village called John Jack. The book gives a flamboyant history told with much dramatic prose and licence, and it becomes annoying at times as it is told in an over-enthusiastic theatrical prose. But he does cover the battle's events in St Monans, and it's from here I got the first mention of the struggle on the beaches. He mentions 600 Englishmen dead on the beaches – "call them foes if you will; while the conquering party, inflated in heart and callous in soul, exulted over their glorious achievement, if carnage, blood, and slaughter be the constituents of glory".

The author, John Jack, goes on to give a story from the field of battle: "one of the Baron's minions, who ... only appeared in the field when the action was over – here sauntering among the dead and dying in the sanguinary theatre (no pleasant prospect for a sensitive mind) brandishing a furbished sword with heroic magnimity, slaying the wounded and wounding the slain, in hopes of appeasing that Baronial indignation which his skulking conduct had kindled. In the exercise of this officious cold-blooded barbarity, he discovered a fine looking young man in officer's uniform, esconced in the shade and shelter of a whinny retreat, where his beautiful spouse, with love's delicate softness, was binding up his bleeding wounds ... whilst a smiling baby, the innocent pledge of their love, was squatted by her side on the cold ground, and playing with its own fingers. The inhuman wretch, with horrid menace, raised his murderous weapon to despatch the wounded man, when the astonished lady, in a paroxysm of feeling, started from the earth and arrested the fury of his arm, imploring mercy for her husband ... while the tears of love and pity gushed from her lovely eyes ... But unmoved by female beauty, and unsoftened by the tears of entreaty, he threw her rudely on the ground and plunged his sword in the bosom of her husband. She shrieked and exclaimed – 'this must be the crook in my lot, of which the astrologer spake before my mother conceived me.' (Hence, that ground is called 'Crook i' the lot' to this day.) The heartless demon still thirsting for blood, despatched the lady."

According to John Jack, the baby was saved by the Baron, and it was eventually found that the bairn's mother belonged to a wealthy family from the English borders, and that she had been determined to follow her officer husand where he was posted, contrary to the wishes of her family. The return of the bairn was requested by the mother's grieving parents, but the Baron refused, bringing up the child in Newark Castle till eventually she married the Baron's eldest son, and ultimately became Lady Newark.

That is John Jack's version of events, witten in 1844, but where he got the information is never given in his book.

The Baron of Newark Castle would have been Sir James Sandilands, but there are no records that mention names of other lesser occupants of the castle which could give realism to this romantic tale. The Sandilands family were to have the castle for another 100 years; they eventually sold the castle to General David Leslie in 1649.

The English on St Monans beach carried a large contingent of marines. In the National Archives at Kew are filed letters dating from the sixteenth century. These include letters from one of the sea captains to Lord Somerset which reveal how bad things were on board. These English had been in Scottish waters for four years terrorising coastal ports and shipping in the "rough wooing". In 1548 Captain Wyndham on the bark *Aiger* is reduced to pleading on behalf of unpaid soldiers and marines, many of whom are ill, as well as asking for more supplies, more men and more ships, so that he can attack the Scots.

On the land at this time an English force was bogged down in trench warfare attempting to take Edinburgh castle as French and Scots army detachments stood in the way. Disease was rife, and plague was scouring the country. We can see Thomas begging for permission to attack the land forces in the Firth, he may have been under pressure to let his men pillage, as a letter of January 12th 1548 reminds Somerset that it is impossible to stop them stealing. From further letters, it seems the sailors on board have not been paid again, as he requests wages once more.* With this long time at sea and money not arriving, keeping order must have been a huge problem, when you think of a ship stacked with men freezing cold under the wooden decks, with no pay for months. I'm sure the thought and promise of raiding the undefended coastline of Fife must have appealed very highly to the sailors for if nothing else the want of booty and plunder. The bark the *Aiger* is on Admiralty records as being 300 tonnes.

It wasn't just the marines who were having a bad time with wages; I have the written will from a Robert Shell from Berwick upon Tweed. He is dying in 1550 but was a master gunner during the

* NOTE: Fascinating transcriptions are to be found in the book *The Navy of Edward VI and Mary I*, by C S Knighton.

Sixteenth-century artillery in action.

years of fighting with the Scots. In his will he is requesting the unpaid wages for him and his servants who fought with him in the battles against the Scottish forces. It reads (modernised slightly): "The 7th of August in the third year of king Edward the sixth – I Robert Shell of Berwick gunner makes this my will and testament in manner and form following first I bequeath my soul to God almighty and to all the celestial company in heaven my body to be buried in the churchyard in Berwick. ... Debts owing to him with money. In reals near 24 pounds. In silver 5 or 6 pounds. In the king's majesty's hands to be paid by Mr Doune for 3 months ended the first of September at eightpence the day for my self and sixpence the day for either of two servants and from the 1st of September unto the 6th of the same at like wages by the space of [four score —] days at twenty pence the day 12 pounds. Mr Ridgway oweth me for work of Dunglasse Home and Roxburgh £3.13.4d. Mr Captane for my wages 12 days at eightpence per diem and for my servants' wages at sixpence per day for 12 days 20 shillings. Also Mr Captane oweth stripping a piece of ordinance and Clement Shell ten shillings and more unto me four shillings. Fourteen shillings. ..." (The will is in the Registry at Durham.)

On the outskirts of Edinburgh, the retreating Scots forces after the battle of Pinkie in late 1547 had dug trenches and manned, walled forts for the defence of Edinburgh. The victorious English never pursued the fleeing Scots army to Edinburgh, and lay relatively inactive at the port of Leith licking their wounds from the battle and savouring the victory. Lord Somerset by the end of 1547 now had garrisons of men at Blackness, and on the islands of Inchcolm and Inchkeith, controlling and defending the English fleet resting here. Broughty Castle at the mouth of the Tay was held and an army was positioned at Dundee, Haddington having the bulk of the forces.

The island of Inchcolm sits today just a few kilometres from the Forth Road Bridge. It's a small island, about 9 hectares. There were fortifications here to deter the German Nazi aircraft during the Second World War if they attacked the Forth Bridge. It's smack in the middle of the waterway, a great location to restrict any transports trying to reach Edinburgh. With cannons at the ready, nothing should get past the island without being assaulted. Lord Seymour could see its importance and had landed a number of men and cannon there. But as with many of Admiral Seymour's decisions, disaster wasn't far away. I turn again to the French officer Jean de Beaugué, who witnessed much of the fighting from 1547–49. The large French force of 6,000 that slipped past the English fleet sitting idle in the Forth had to deal with the island of Inchcolm; this is how Jean describes the assault:

"All our soldiers landed with much difficulty, meeting great resistance. But when the fighting began on the island and Monsieur de Dessé and his men joined battle, the enemy took fright on seeing their general struck down and killed before their eyes, that same general who had not long ago before caused the death of Desbroyes. Their fright was such that they put up no more resistance but retreated in disorder to the tip of the island where they were all captured like sheep. I do not wish to recall the fear the English had in the face of death. 'For I consider that other men's fear, being something so unworthy of a soldier, should not be set before the eyes of young men who make profession of valour and virtue.' I can say that, with the loss of only two men, we captured Inchcolm from the English who numbered more than 800 seasoned, experienced soldiers, while we had less than 700 to give them battle. We found there a good quantity of medium and heavy artillery, stocks of food and munitions, and all sorts of tools and materials to fortify the island, together with a large transport ship, loaded with Malmsey, cross-bolts, silk and woollen cloth, and other items required to garrison and fortify a place of great strategic importance. In this connection I must say that, off all the nations in the world, the English are those that take the greatest care in provisioning the forts which they capture, but they are also bad at holding them. Monsieur de Dessé refused to take a share of the booty captured on the island, saying to those who endeavoured to make him change his mind that he would never take for himself the things which should belong to the soldiers as a reward for their deeds of valour. 'I myself,' he said, 'have never wished to return to France enriched with anything other than glory.' Truly these words were spoken by a generous heart which sought honour alone as reward for its valour."

I have spent some time myself on Inchcolm island back in the 1980s and it certainly could accommodate the 800 English Jean de Beaugué states were here. The island had an abbey that would have been standing in 1548 – probably where the English were barracked. Losing the island was a huge strategic loss and any English ships trying to reach Edinburgh would now be under direct cannon fire. It was another letdown by the inefficient English navy that they couldn't intercept the French as they sneaked past them in the Firth of Forth and that the island was given up so easily. While the English Admiral Thomas Seymour had more than forty ships blockading the Firth of Forth, the Scottish Queen Mary sailed from the west coast to Brest in France, travelling on to Laon, and an eventual marriage with the French dauphin, the heir to the throne.

According to Lyndesay of Pitscottie, "But this is to be remembered, that whilst the siege remained at Haddington, by a convention or assembly of the lords, it was decreed that the queen should be sent into France. And thereupon Monsieur de Villegaignon, with four galleys departed from Leith, made semblance as if he would have sailed into France; but having passed the mouth of the Forth, he turned his course on the left-hand, to pass almost the shore northward by the German Seas, that compassing the land on the east-side, he might pass about by the Isle of Orkney, and so by the West Isles, till he came to Dumbarton, where the young queen lay. This journey he fortunately achieved, the same never before (to man's remembrance) being made or attempted with galleys."

Worse still, a French relief force of 6,000 men arrived, unmolested by the English navy under Lord Seymour's watch, which was supposed to be protecting Leith, and landed soldiers there on 16 June 1548 (just before the attack at St Monans) to take up arms in the trench warfare around Edinburgh, strengthening the Scots' resolve. The English fleet did intercept and capture a number of the departing French ships, but they had already offloaded their soldiers at Leith.

It was now obvious to Lord Somerset that there would be no match between King Edward VI and

Mary Queen of Scots, no matter how rough the wooing went! If only he had pursued the retreating Scots forces through to Edinburgh after the battle of Pinkie, Queen Mary had been at Holyrood House and could have been captured. But no matter how well the land forces were doing, it was all being undone by Admiral Seymour's lacklustre efforts in letting the French get away with Queen Mary. The two disastrous landings in St Monans and Montrose had cost nearly 1,500 lives with at least 1,000 captured and a ship lost, and now the landing of the French army at Edinburgh sealed his fate! With the navy so ineffective, the admiral was recalled to London in disgrace.

Chapter Seven

Those Who Died

From the evidence I have unearthed from the sources mentioned so far, there was indeed a mighty battle fought in the vicinity of the beachhead at St Monans. In French, English and Scottish sources, there are snippets of the battle. And in all the reports we find between 600 and 900 slain English!

There's no mention anywhere of the Scottish dead, but here is my problem ... let's say at the least estimate "600 dead" on the battlefield ... that is a hell of a size of grave to dig!

According to John Jack, in his *History of St Monance*, in 1827, major alterations, renovations and decorations of the kirk were projected, and while it was undergoing the alterations, "there was such an exposure made of the mouldering ruins of humanity as has seldom been the lot of mortal eyes to witness. A vast quantity of the bones and ashes of former generations was applied as manure to the farm of Newark, which so enriched the soil that it produced little or nothing for several years. This was merely the agricultural view of the cause which produced the singular sterility of the soil ..." Could this perhaps be the remains of the English dead?

In this manner the Scottish general Leslie's remains were dug up and with many others cast into the sea. The bodies of the men of rank, men with titles, killed in the battle would be ransomed or claimed by their wealthy families as was the custom, and good money could be made from it.

But the common soldiers would have no such luxury, nothing but a communal grave. But they are the ones I am interested in – where would their grave be? Obviously the church has a graveyard, but you would think that any burial on that scale would be recorded, and would be noted by many parties, and not be forgotten in folklore. Unfortunately the Register of the Privy Council of this period is not preserved for us to read further.

Another example in our history makes me think that the burials of the common people were not always remembered. Take the soldiers who fought with Leslie at the battle of Dunbar in

1650. After the execution of Charles I in 1649 his son was proclaimed King Charles II almost immediately. It took eighteen months to get him from the safety of France to Scotland, but he came under oath, to embrace Presbyterianism and to root out episcopacy. These were all the details that his father refused to adhere to – it had cost him civil war from 1642 to 1646 and, in 1649, his head.

David Leslie, owner of Newark Castle, was now head of the Scottish army and so had a role in the war which led to Cromwell's victory over Charles II. The Scots took up arms for the king, and Oliver Cromwell immediately in person landed with an army to deal with the threat. With disease rife, Cromwell's army retreated from Leslie's army and looked finally beaten and stuck on Dunbar beach. Surrounded by Leslie's force it looked very bleak for Cromwell – for the first time in his military career he looked beaten. All Leslie had to do, with having the high ground, was to keep Cromwell from coming off his lowland position and let the disease reduce his men. Leslie had 22,000 men to Cromwell's compact and disease-ridden 12,000. Cromwell was losing men to disease and was about to capitulate when, to his amazement, the Scottish forces started to

Oliver Cromwell at the battle of Dunbar in 1650.

disengage and come down from the high ground, with church ministers leading the men – brandishing nothing but crosses at Cromwell's men.

Leslie had lost command. Seeing a defeated foe on the beach, the ministers tried to steal the glory away from Leslie and make it a victory for God.

The Committee of the Kirk thought that Cromwell (or Agag, as they liked to call him) had embarked half his men and half his guns, when he had only shipped off his sick and wounded, and instead of letting Leslie wait for the surrender of Cromwell, whose army was afflicted by famine and sickness, the clergy exhorted the Scots soldiers to "march down in the might of the Most High" and reminded them how Gideon had wrought salvation for Israel. On top of that, they insisted on purging the army of 4,000 "malignants", in other words, prohibiting any of the oldest and most experienced soldiers from taking part in the action.

Oliver Cromwell couldn't believe what he saw, and neither could Leslie! Cromwell exclaimed, "They are coming! They are coming down! The Lord hath delivered them into our hands!" The ministers led the army, waving crosses at the English, bringing the army down from the advantage of the high ground to meet the trapped and desperate English forces on the beach. The English just couldn't believe what they were witnessing. The Scots coming down from the heights, from a position previously all to the Scots' advantage, so that their force was now disjointed and their solid formation all scattered.

According to Captain Hodgson, Cromwell is supposed to have exclaimed: "Let God arise, and let His enemies be scattered! Like as the mist vanisheth, so shalt Thou drive them away!"

Both sides were strongly motivated by religious beliefs. The watchword of the Scots was "Scotland and the Covenant", that of the English was, "The Lord of Hosts".

The English ironsides attacked and what ensued was total chaos and destruction of the Scottish army. With Leslie unable to keep his men in check, he also retreated, leaving 3,000 dead and as many as 10,000 prisoners. If the church had not interfered in matters, it is fairly certain history today would have been changed, with Charles II on the throne ten years earlier and Leslie the man who finally humbled the great warrior Oliver Cromwell.

With the disaster of the battle of Dunbar in 1650, the Scots Commander David Leslie escaped with his officers and much of the cavalry away from the carnage of the Dunbar battlefield.

The battle was described by Oliver Cromwell in his letters as being "a total rout", with 3,000 Scots dead on the field. He described what was taken on the battlefield: many prisoners, including about 10,000 private soldiers – "the whole baggage and train taken, wherein was good store of match, powder and bullet; all their artillery,

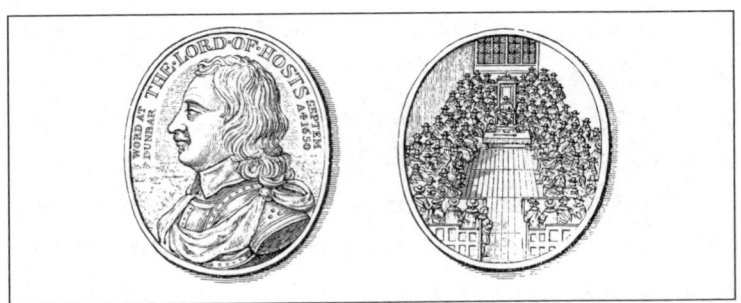

Both sides claimed God's support. After Oliver Cromwell's unexpected victory at Dunbar, the English House of Commons voted for these gold and silver medals to be distributed among their officers and soldiers who had fought there.

great and small – thirty guns. We are confident they have left behind not less than fifteen thousand arms ... I do not believe we have lost 20 men ... Thus you have the prospect of one of the most signal mercies God hath done for England and his people, this war." *

For the Scots prisoners, it was a long treacherous walk south to English jails and eventual deportation for many to the American colonies. In 2013, a mass grave was uncovered in Durham. It was examined and after researchers examined the skeletons, they concluded they were victims of the battle of Dunbar. The bodies were identified as all male and between 13 and 25 years old – prisoners

* NOTE: Cromwell's letter is quoted under 'Dunbar' in *The Gazetteer of Scotland* 1844.

of the march south from the battlefield of Dunbar after 3 September 1650. An estimated 1,000 of the Scots prisoners are believed to have died on the march south to Durham. It was thought this was the burial ground for soldiers who died at Durham. Some were executed, others died from wounds and dysentery. Records state that 3,000 prisoners were kept at the cathedral and castle here for a while.

Two giant burial grounds were discovered. Initial analysis suggested the deaths predated the battle of Dunbar, but research continued. Some of the bodies had clay pipes commonly used in Scotland and isotope analysis showed the skeletons were probably of Scottish origin. Dating analysis suggested deaths between 1625 and 1660. Andrew Millard, senior lecturer at the Durham Department of Archaeology, said that the only plausible explanation of the evidence was that these were the Scottish soldiers from the battle of Dunbar.

Richard Annis, senior archaeologist with Durham University, said that it was a significant find, because it shed new light on what happened to the bodies of the Scottish soldiers after the battle. He said it was possible there were more mass graves under buildings of the University of

Durham, areas which would not have been built on back in the middle of the 17th century.

General David Leslie was to be given the title Lord Newark after the restoration of Charles II. The title came from his castle in St Monans, and he would reside there till his death in 1682. He was buried in the church ground and lay there peacefully until the 1800s, when his bones were unceremoniously dumped into the sea during a rebuilding project.

With Leslie losing at Dunbar on 3rd September 1650 the remaining Scottish forces joined the English supporters of Charles II at Worcester on 29th August 1651, where Charles II's hopes were smashed by Cromwell's ironsides. The outcome would have the generals of the king's force either beheaded or imprisoned; Leslie was captured and would be imprisoned for several years. It would lead to Oliver Cromwell being sworn in as the first Lord Protector of the Commonwealth of England, Scotland and Ireland. An English army would occupy Scotland for the next few years. Peace of a sort was now obtained after seven years of constant fighting.

During the English occupation by Cromwell's forces in Scotland from 1651 to 1660, a huge amount of parish records and Scottish accounts were removed by the English forces and taken to the Tower of London for safekeeping. With the ascent to the throne of Charles II in 1660 after the death of Cromwell in 1658, the Scottish records were returned. But one ship called the *Elizabeth*, loaded with records, foundered off the coast of Newcastle and sank, taking lots of first-account parish records to a watery grave lost forever. The St Monans parish records and the intimate details of the battle of St Monans could have been in this ship!

It's my belief that the dissolution of the monasteries in 1559 and the English occupation of 100 years later were the reasons that "The battle of St Monans" has been forgotten in history. It was much more than a simple skirmish, but was preserved only in the memories of the veterans who fought it. The quick succession of deaths and executions and assassinations of the main leaders of the battle in 1548 quickly stopped any such time for celebratory stories of glory. And the beaten English were in no hurry at all to boast of two sound defeats.

Today the national records of Scotland are held in Princes Street, Edinburgh. The earliest files are from 1189 called *The Quitclaim of Canterbury*. The records have shared Scotland's turbulent history.

First they were held in dry, decent conditions in Stirling Castle till 1651, when Oliver Cromwell had them removed and taken to the Tower of London. But not all files made it; some were stolen by clerks and by the English garrison left in Stirling. The Scottish records were returned in 1660, but as we know, the English ships bringing home the mass of files hit a huge storm, the *Elizabeth* came to grief in the waters off Northumberland and many records from the Scottish archives were lost forever! The ones that survived the journey north were taken to Edinburgh Castle for safekeeping, then in 1662 to Laigh Hall, below the Parliament Hall, on the Royal Mile.

The records that had survived were finally all delivered here in 1689, but this location for such fragile papers was a mistake! It was vermin-infested and very damp, and a huge fire in the area in 1700 put the records at risk again, so they were taken to St Giles Church in Edinburgh where it was thought to be drier and more convenient.

A permanent home for the Scottish records was found in 1765, funded from confiscated Jacobite estates after the failure of Charles Edward Stewart's attempt to put his family back on the throne.

The famous architect Robert Adam started work on building a new office for them but by

1779 the funds had totally run out. Construction started up again in 1820 and the building was finally opened in 1847. Today the General Register House still stands in Princes Street. With all the moving, the fires and vessels coming to grief with the Scottish records, it's a surprise we have only lost some of the years of Mary Queen of Scots' reign and her regents' turbulent histories. My attempts to retell this story of the St Monans battle have come mostly from contemporary accounts. There is no James Stewart version, no Sir John Wemyss account, or anything from the lairds of Largo. But these men would all be dead before long, as would the English admiral.

Recently there was an archaeological dig on and around the site of the now ruined castle of Newark by St Andrews archaeologist Edwina Proudfoot, who excavated a small part of the area with her team. I was lucky enough to get her thoughts on whether there could be a burial ground of a large size in the immediate area, but unfortunately her small dig was confined to the inside of the castle walls, and no other such dig was approved. She could not help at all with thoughts of a larger burial ground around the castle, but elevated views of the area show a disruption in the grasslands, west of the castle

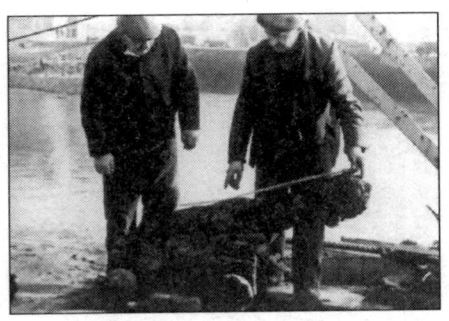

In the 1970s an old cannon was caught in the nets of a local fishing boat and landed at St Monans.

by two hundred metres. That would be a perfect position for depositing bodies of those who had died in the struggle to get back on the English ships at the sea edge. But until someone excavates this portion of land again, it is all guesswork.

My old friend Brian Watson lived in Pittenweem (he was once the harbour master there); he was an eager metal detectorist. He would survey the Newark Castle areas every year, finding medieval pendants from war horses giving proof of the castle's military past. He once found a golden badge, in the shape of a shell, which was recognized by experts as being a pilgrim badge from Spain. Perhaps a monk on a pilgrimage to St Andrews had dropped it, probably staying in Templars' accommodation and

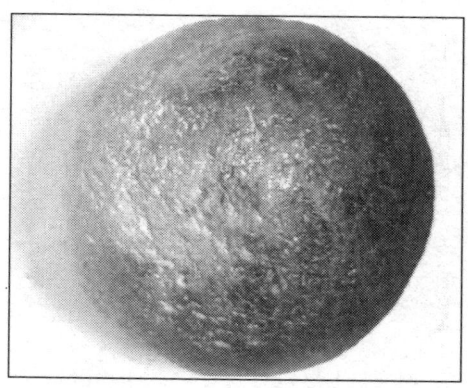

One of Brian Watson's cannonball finds.

castles en route, and so the badge had fallen near Newark Castle.

Among other things in Brian's collections were hundreds of lead musket and arquebus balls found around the immediate area of the castle. He also found some 10-centimetre lead balls, possibly suiting a small ordnance which a ship might carry. Or could they be cannonballs from Sir John Wemyss' three small ordnance pieces which fired on the English? The shot is probably too small for the English cannon fired in 1544 by Captain Poyntz's squadrons that set the monastery at St Monans on fire.

Chapter Eight

What Happened to the Participants

By far the most prominent characters in the battle of St Monans on the English side were Admiral Thomas Seymour, and Edward Seymour Lord Somerset.

Thomas Seymour

Thomas Seymour's exploits in Scotland in 1548 and the disasters of his ill-led incursions at St Monans and Montrose left him politically exposed. The loss of the grounded ship at St Monans and the dead he left on the two beaches, maybe as many as 2,000, had to be funded from the crown's resources. Thousands of sailors on the sixty ships involved in Scotland had to be funded even if they sat idle as the French fleet outmanoeuvred them. Events brought him back to the English

Admiralty in shame. While his huge navy sailed in Fife waters, the French naval force had succeeded in taking on board the young Mary Queen of Scots at Dumbarton, on the west coast of Scotland. They had sailed away completely unmolested by English gunnery, safely delivering her to Scotland's ally France.

It was a damning disgrace: the whole point of the land and sea expedition had been to force the marriage of Mary Queen of Scots and Edward of England. Although the land forces had done well, the navy had been nothing less than a disaster. The admiral's status downtrodden, he had arrived back in shame in England to be met by more bad tidings. It was the news that his wife, Catherine Parr (the widow of Henry VIII) had died on 5th September 1548.

For Thomas Seymour, 1548 had been his disaster of a year. He was friendless, and now with his wife's death he had lost all influence in court. He held only a guardian's position over his royal nephew, but with this power base he tried to finance a rebellion against the young King Edward's advisors. His position of admiral was weakened, but he thought he could raise at least 10,000 fighting men towards his bid for power.

Seymour was willing to chance it all on a move as rash as his landings in St Monans – an attempt to kidnap the young king and then hold him for ransom, a caper which led to him being caught one night in the gardens of the king's house at Kensington Palace.

The attempt failed when he disturbed the king's dog. Creeping around the gardens of Kensington House at nightfall trying to find the young king's bedchamber, Seymour woke up the dogs! The spaniels made so much racket Thomas Seymour took his pistol and shot one of the noisy beasts dead! The foolishly thought-out action and the discharge of the weapon could not fail to bring out the castle guards, and he was instantly arrested.

A special session of parliament was held on 4 November 1549. It was decided to proceed against Seymour for treason by bill of attainder. This was a parliamentary way of destroying him without going to the trouble and risk of giving him a trial. After heavy persuasion, the young king agreed to this procedure, and that counted for a great deal. The House of Lords saw no problem when the bill was laid before it, and it was passed without objection. There were some reservations in the House of Commons. Some members even objected against the method of proceeding by a bill of attainder passed in absence of the king, maintaining that a formal trial ought to be given to every man before his condemnation.

But on 20 March 1550 a message came to Parliament from Edward, pressing the House of Commons to proceed with the bill, and pointing out that the information provided to them had satisfied the Lords. They were persuaded to go along with the king's wishes, and the bill was passed by nearly 400 votes to a mere nine or ten dissenters. The sentence of death was carried out without delay, and Thomas Seymour was taken and beheaded on London's Tower Hill, aged forty.

Edward Seymour

Edward Seymour, Lord Somerset, was the older brother of Thomas. His efforts in Scotland fell into a stalemate because of Scots and French resistance and his brother's poor show as admiral. When Somerset was in Scotland during this stalemate in 1549, a rebellion was started by peasants over land rights in Norfolk, led by Robert Kett. Somerset took the English army back into England to deal with the problem, but he became engaged in political turmoil threatening the English Council, now run by John Dudley, Earl of Warwick, who was leader of the king's court. Edward Seymour fell into conflict with John Dudley, and was soon charged with felony and scheming to overthrow the court. Edward, like his brother Thomas before him, was beheaded on Tower Hill in London in January 1552.

Lord Clinton

Lord Edward Clinton commanded the English navy during Edward Seymour's invasion of Scotland in 1547. At the request of Admiral Seymour he attacked Fife in 1548, with disastrous consequences for the admiral. According to some reports, Clinton was lucky to get off St Monans beach alive. He would replace the admiral in 1550 after Seymour's arrest, and keep that position for three years. He raided the French coasts with the English fleet in 1588 and was created the Earl of Lincoln. He served three English monarchs ... Henry VIII, Edward VI and Queen Elizabeth. He was an ambassador for Queen Elizabeth to the French up to his death in 1585.

Nicholas Poyntz

Nicholas was a great family friend of Admiral Seymour. He fell from grace when Lord Seymour the admiral was arrested. He was jailed in the

Tower of London for a year simply for his close connections to Thomas Seymour, but no evidence could be found to show that Poyntz was anything to do with the rebellion planned by Seymour (during the time Poyntz spent in jail, Lord Seymour was beheaded).

Nicholas Poyntz was subsequently released and he died in his family home in 1556 – of a fever.

The Scottish participants in the St Monans and Montrose landings ...

James Stewart 1st Earl of Moray

He remained an important figure in Scotland. Lord James Stewart was Queen Mary's advisor after her return from France in 1561, and he led a royal force on her behalf against the 4th Earl of Huntly, who took offence at Mary when she turned down his son's attentions for marriage. A rebellion started and the Earl of Huntly's Gordon Highlanders were put down by Moray's forces at the battle of Corrichie. A supporter of the Reformation, he was nevertheless made Earl of Moray by her in 1562.

Civil war broke out between on the one hand Queen Mary's forces and supporters and on the

Mary Queen of Scots

other hand her second husband Darnley (Henry Stewart). James Stewart supported the rebels and the Queen was forced to abdicate in favour of her son, who would eventually be crowned James VI and I of Britain.

After Mary Queen of Scots abdicated, James Stewart, Earl of Moray, was appointed Regent on 22 August 1567, looking after the young king who was just over one year old, and who had been crowned King James VI of Scotland on 24th July 1567.

James Stewart's life would last only a few more years, being brought to a violent end when he was assassinated in the town of Linlithgow, shot dead in his carriage by James Hamilton (a Queen Mary supporter). He has a grave in St Giles cathedral in Edinburgh. He was buried on 14 February 1570, and John Knox gave the sermon over his good friend.

Born out of wedlock, James Stewart was a valiant and resourceful man. History in Scotland would look different now had he been born legitimate. He certainly had the manner and intelligence to have been a great king.

John Wood

After the battle John Wood formed a great friendship with James Stewart, following him to Queen Mary's wedding in France to the dauphin who became King Francis II, but who would only live two years more! When Queen Mary came back from France, John Wood acted as her half-brother's secretary. When James Stewart became Earl of Moray, Wood was to act as emissary and deliver the earl's letters, becoming a frequent visitor to the English courts. It was on one of those visits that he carried a casket of secret and damning letters showing that Queen Mary had been involved in the death of her husband Lord Darnley.

In 1562, he became senator of the College of Justice and was made Lord of Tullidavie. When

Queen Mary married the Earl of Bothwell in 1567, civil war broke out. John Wood took the regent James Stewart's side against Mary. In 1570 Wood was attacked in the countryside of Fife: he was shot, assassinated on 15 April by the Laird of Kilquonquar and his son Arthur Forbes. Both were supporters of Queen Mary. In George Buchanan's *Admonition to the True Lords* it is stated that John Wood was slain for no other cause, but for being a good servant to the crown and to the regent his master.

John Erskine of Dun

Erskine was Provost of Montrose at the time of the assault by the English on Montrose beach. He was a good friend of Regent James Stewart. He was appointed on 26th June 1558 by Parliament to be a commissioner to France.

He was one of the Scottish ambassadors sent to witness Queen Mary of Scots' marriage to the dauphin in France, with John Wood. On his return from this business, assassins made an attempt on his life with poison as he waited in Dieppe. Four of his closest friends would die from the poisoned wine but John Erskine survived the attempt. Although James Stewart and John Wood were assassinated, this particular attempt failed. At this time Scotland was at peace with England, and the assassins may have been Catholic dissenters. He sailed back to Scotland supporting the Protestant movement and became a supporter and friend of John Knox. He lived a long life in office at Montrose dying in 1591.

James Sandilands

As the owner of Newark Castle he had no great military might, but mustered every man who could carry weapons to fight the invader from his lands. He died in 1585 and the castle was inherited by his grandson Sir William Sandilands. James was a good friend of John Knox and endorsed the Protestant movement, dislodging the Benedictine monks from St Monans church in 1560. Newark Castle would stay with the Sandilands family for amother 100 years and be sold in 1649 to Lieutenant General David Leslie.

The man who had to sell the castle to pay his debts was Lord Abercrombie (also named James Sandilands). He was said to have betrayed his ancestors – a wastrel who lived riotously.

Sir John Wemyss

From the 24th to the 28th July 1547 the Queen Dowager had stayed at Wemyss castle as a guest.

Sir John Wemyss entertained her daughter Mary Queen of Scots in February 1564 in the same castle, where she would meet her future husband Lord Darnley. He would remain loyal to her, fighting at the battle of Langside on the 13th May 1568. He lived till 1572.

That's the battle of St Monans, told from the sides that fought it from all the accounts I can find from 1548 and near that time. From what I've uncovered here it was a mighty struggle that involved thousands of fighting men and it should reclaim its place in the history books as a great victory for the Scots. A great victory over the Auld Enemy at a time when we had suffered our worst defeat from them at Pinkie, but if you read the previous participants of the struggle not many of the leaders from both sides lived long after the battle. This event should be taught in the schools and talked around this coastline with pride that our ancestors once fought and died for this soil we call Scotland!

Appendix

For the interested reader, the following pages hold the complete account of the battle on St Monans beach in 1548 from the writings of the Bishop of Ross, and this is the most descriptive source we have. John Lesley's account was published in Latin in his *The History of Scotland*. The Scots original of the second half of his work was handed to Mary Queen of Scots as a gift.

The Scots version was published in 1830 by the Bannatyne Club. In a preliminary notice pulished in their edition, it was explained that although Bishop Lesley's *History of Scotland* was first published in Rome in Latin in 1578, the second part of his book (covering the period from 1436 to 1562) was originally written in the Scots language for Mary Queen of Scots, intended to sustain her fortitude and constancy. He presented this manuscript in Scots to the Queen in 1571, and two years later left Scotland for the Continent. The original manuscript has been lost, but it is possible that after the execution of Mary Queen of Scots it remained in the possession of Sir Andrew Melville of Garvock, her Master of Household, the brother of Sir Robert Melville of Murdocairnie, created Lord Melville in 1616, and of Sir James Melville of Halhill. It is likely that one of the Melville brothers had a transcript made, for the earliest copy to survive belonged to the Melville family. It could have been taken for the Queen's original copy, were it not for some errors in transcription, especially in proper names. The manuscript, which was provided to the Bannatyne Club editor by the Earl of Leven and Melville, survived in a mutilated state, and the gaps were filled by using a later copy, probably from the early 17th century, which is in the Bodleian Library. The introduction to the Bannatyne Club edition describes the book as "a specimen of pure and vigorous composition, in his native language, by one of the most able and accomplished Scotchmen of the sixteenth century".

The text is in old Scots, and the letter 'f' was used as an 's' which would probably confuse today's reader somewhat, so I have changed that. Otherwise I have stayed loyal to the text as it was written; for some outdated words I have explained the meanings in brackets.

John Lesley, Bishop of Ross

At the same time the Inglis (English) flotte (fleet) entering into the frith sought occasioun to haif gevin ayd to the land army, in case they had joyned in battell with the Scottis and Frenche men. Bot perceaving no good to be done that way, thay tuik in hand uther interprises; and thairfoir thay determinat to lande a certain nowmer of thair men on the north syd of the frithe, to make sum spoil within the cuntrey of Fyif. Bot the Larde of Wemis, as than being sum quhat seiklie [ill], and thairfoir returned hame frome the campt, caused suche watche and wairde dalie [daily] and nychtlie [nightly] to be keped, that the admirall of Inglande culd not convoye his interprice so secretlie bot that the same was perceaved; for it happinit so that the laird of Wemis, that same nycht the admirall purposed to cum to lande, he come doune him selfe to serche the watche befoir day; and perceaving the lycht quhilk [which] the Inglismen had in their shippes, as than wisse [wish] to set thair men aland, quhairupoun douting the worst, (a thing that sendill [seldom] brings repentance,) with all diligence he tuik ordour for the calling furth of so mony men as cud be maid ather [either] within the toun of Sank Minanis, quhilk was not abone the nowmer of sax scoir [120] men, or neir thare aboutis; and having bestowed thame in syndre places quhair he thought neidfull, he schowsed [chose] furth a certane nowmer of the most practised, and went with them doune to the place quhair he had sene the lycht, a ij [2] miles of [off] frome the toun of Sanct Minanis, to onderstand quhat the matter mycht meane; and be reasone that it was towardis day it waxit [grew] mirker [darker] than it had bene of all the nycht befoir, swa that he come so neir to the ennemyis, that he baith hard and saw ther manner aweill as he could wishe to doo; quhilk done he shortlie [quickly] returned to his company agane, and putting thame in the best ordour he culd, awaiting the ennemy at thair first approcheing, which was in the brek of the day, thay war receaved at the first schot of arrowis, and handlit for a quhile with scarmushis [skirmishes] rycht sharplie; bot according to the appointment in that case devysed, at lenth the Scottismen retiret within certane trinches, qhuair thay kendillit [kindled] certane fairins [ferns], stray [straw] and uther thingis prepared for the purpois, and maid ane mervelous gret reik [smoke] and fuilbik [fell back?]; and thair thay had thre small peaces of small artailyerie, quhilkis thay discharged so directly apoun the Inglismen, that they shafed [sliced up?] thame quhilk first fell in scarmushing with thame, that no small nowmer of Inglismen were slayne; whil Laird Wemis with that company quhilk he had with him in the trinches, set upoun the ennemyis afrount with a gret fureous noyce, dinging [striking] thame doun on heapes; bot also ane uther company quhilk wer send to fetche a compas [circuit] behind the back of ane hill began to shaw thame selffis [themselves], making sic ane hidderous noise and cry as thocht thay walde haif borne doun all befoir thame; and yit that band was bot of the meaner sort of peple, princepallie wemen and childrene, leaste abill to work any great feat; notwithstanding for that, alsweill thay appered to be licklie [brave looking] men, and well appointed for the war. The Inglismen not perceaving the fraud, tuik thame to thair helis and fled towart thair shippes, skattered heir and thair without ordour; quhome the Scottis followed in close evin hard to the wattir syd, and slew divers of thame within the watter or thay mycht recover thair boittis [boats]. Of ane thousand that come alande, thay not returned not three hundreth back agane to thair shippes, bot was oder [either] drownit or slayne. The admirall him self hardlie eskaped to his shipp, commandit the saylis to be heised [hoisted] up, and so departed without longer tarie thair for that tyme.

This owrthrow of the Inglis men, was the occasione that thay never preassed [attempted] thaireftir to lande in Fife during all the tyme of the warris.

Sources

Breviarium Aberdonense 1509

Calendar of State Papers relating to Scotland, Letters 1509–1589

Gazetteer of Scotland 1844 vols 1 and 2

Wills and Inventories from the Registry at Durham

Collections relating to the History of Mary Queen of Scots, 3 volumes, James Anderson 1727

An English Garner: Tudor Tracts 1532–88, Edward Arber

Annales of Scotland, James Balfour 1630, published 1824

The Shores of Fife, William Ballingal 1872

A Calendar of Scottish Saints, Dom Michael Barrett O.S.B. 1919

The History of the Campagnes 1548 and 1549, Jean de Beaugué

Scotichronicon, Walter Bower (d. 1449) ed. Goodall 1759

Admonition to the True Lords, George Buchanan 1571, republished 1823

History of Scotland, George Buchanan 1582

The History of the Kirk of Scotland, David Calderwood 1842

The Scottish Correspondence of Mary of Lorraine, ed Annie I. Cameron 1927

Tudor Sea Power, David Childs 2009

A Treatise on the Law of Scotland Respecting Tithes, Sir John Connell 1815

Annals of Pittenweem, David Cook 1840

The Pictorial History of England, George L. Craik and Charles MacFarlane, 1838

Memorials of the Family of Wemyss of Wemyss, Sir William Fraser 1888

A Commentary of the Services and Charges of William Lord Grey of Wilton, Arthur Lord Grey of Wilton (1567–77), edited by Sir Philip Malpas Grey Egerton 1847

History of the Reign of Mary Queen of Scots, Lord Herris 1836

The Scottish Chronicle, or A Complete History and Description of Scotland, Raphael Hollinshead 1805

History of St Monance, John Jack 1844

The Navy of Edward VI and Mary I, C. S. Knighton 2011

History of Scotland 1436–1565, Robert Lyndesay (written in the 16th century) 1728

History of England, Mrs Markham (Elizabeth Penrose) 1844

The Expedicion into Scotlande, William Patten 1548

Criminal Trials in Scotland Vol I 1488–1568, Robert Pitcairn 1833

The History of Scotland in the Reigns of Queen Mary and King James VI, William Robertson 1787

Life of John Erskine of Dun, 1508–1591, Scoto-Britannico (Mary Webster) 1879

Battles in Britain 1066–1746 William Seymour 1975

Statistical Account of Scotland, J Sinclair vol X 1791–1799

A History of the Church of Scotland – vol II, John Spottiswoode 1655, republished 1851

The Pictorial History of Scotland AD79–1746, James Taylor 1859

History of the Scottish People Vol 3, Rev Thomas Thomson 1895

Also by Leonard Low
from Steve Savage Publishers

The Weem Witch

'The most complete account yet of the suffering inflicted upon the unfortunate victims of the anti-witch hysteria which gripped local communities in the 17th and 18th centuries ... the remarkable stories he has uncovered are fascinating, enriched as they are by a dense assortment of facts and personal accounts which are as gripping as they are enlightening '
— *East Fife Mail*

ISBN 9781904246190 RRP £9.95

Largo's Untold Stories

Adventure, drama, disaster, at home and in faraway lands, yet all connected with one small community ...

ISBN 9781904246398 RRP £9.95

St Andrews' Untold Stories

'A topic he's quite passionate about ... fascinating ... fans of Len's other books will be glad to know there's some witch stories in there too.'
— *Fife Today*

ISBN 9781904246442 RRP £9.95

Available from bookshops or directly from the publisher.

For information on mail order terms, see our website (www.savagepublishers.com) or write to: Mail Order Dept., Steve Savage Publishers Ltd., The Old Truman Brewery, 91 Brick Lane, LONDON, E1 6QL.

Also from Steve Savage Publishers

Lewis
A History of the Island
Donald Macdonald

A history that covers every aspect of life from prehistory through the Norse period, the clan feuds and the various proprietorships up until recent times.

ISBN 9781904246087 RRP £12.50

Orkney from Old Photographs
Gordon Wright

'A faithful and comprehensive representation of Orcadian life from the 1860s to the 1930s'
—*The Scots Magazine*

ISBN 9781904246244 RRP £14.50

Clan Gregor
Forbes Macgregor

The fascinating story of the MacGregors' struggle to maintain their position in the face of the ambitions of other Scottish clans.

ISBN 9781904246374 RRP £7.50

The Place Names of Edinburgh
Stuart Harris

A massive, groundbreaking work that details the names, old and new, of thousands of streets, roads, villages, hills and other places within modern Edinburgh.

ISBN 9781904246060 RRP £29.50